Knowing By Heart

Authorship & Pen Name

Lee Whitney wrote as "Jacob Erdman" for the *Kings County Record* for over three decades.

The essays in this book have been composed from the archive of his weekly columns, which were published under the heading "A Letter From Home."

Knowing By Heart

A Tribute To A Kennebecasis Valley Homestead Farm

Lee Whitney

with illustrations by
Alice Whitney & Stefan Westner

Chapel Street Editions

Published by
Chapel Street Editions
150 Chapel Street
Woodstock, New Brunswick E7M 1H4
www.chapelstreeteditions.com

ISBN 978-1-988299-27-3

Library and Archives Canada Cataloguing in Publication
Title: Knowing by heart : a tribute to a Kennebecasis Valley homestead farm / Lee Whitney ; with illustrations by Alice Whitney & Stefan Westner
Names: Whitney, Lee, 1935- author.
Description: Lee Whitney wrote as "Jacob Erdman" for the Kings County Record for over three decades. The essays in this book have been composed from the archive of his weekly columns, which were published under the heading "A Letter From Home."
Identifiers: Canadiana 2019021452X | ISBN 9781988299273 (softcover)
Subjects: LCSH: Whitney, Lee, 1935- | LCSH: Whitney, Lee, 1935-— Family. | LCSH: Frontier and pioneer life—New Brunswick—King's County. | LCSH: Farms, Small—New Brunswick—King's County. | LCSH: Farm life—New Brunswick—King's County. | LCSH: King's County (N.B.)—Biography.
Classification: LCC FC2495.K54 Z49 2019 | DDC 971.5/41—dc23

The painting on the cover is by Alice Whitney.

The block-prints and screen-prints throughout the book are by Stefan Westner.

Book design by Brendan Helmuth.

Dedication

To the two and four-legged family members on the farm, without whom these stories would never have been written. And always, for Alice.

Contents

Foreword

When Lee asked me to write these comments, a picture sprang readily and happily to my mind. It was of eating a meal with Lee and his wife Alice in their (then) home outside Sussex, New Brunswick. It was autumn and leaves tumbled down outside the window. Everything was quiet out there; the only sound was that of a cat purring somewhere near our dining table. Lee said, "Let's say grace," but I already knew God was looking gladly down on this peaceful scene.

I met Lee when I was editing the local paper in Sussex, NB—the *Kings County Record*, Canada's oldest continuously published weekly paper. I was always searching frantically for something readable for this farming community whose tastes weren't easy to assess. Dissatisfied readers were apt to turn up at the paper's front counter to give the editor a piece of his or her mind.

"A good read, where did you find him?" a white-haired customer asked, that first week, Lee's opening column neatly cut out and folded in his hand.

"In Apohaqui, originally from the States, by way of Toronto. He and his large family landed here, and have taken up farming, as an escape from city life." I said.

"Good thing. Keep him on," observed the reader. "Can you let me have another copy of this week's paper and I can send a copy to my cousin in the States; it's the sort of thing she reads."

That was so many years ago, and readers continued to follow Lee's weekly column (written under the name of Jacob Erdman) for another 30 years. In those columns, week by week, he painted pictures of rural New Brunswick and life on a small farm, capturing the family's "come-from-away" adventures while, in the process, fashioning observant, sometimes hilarious snapshots, with a deft touch and a humorous and kindly eye.

As Alice observed of their long-ago decision to "stay put" here in New Brunswick, "we've never looked back." Indeed, readers were glad the author and his family decided to stay and take their chances.

Ann Farrell
former editor of the *Kings County Record*

Preface

I had wanted for some time to compile a book from the columns I had written over the years for the *Kings County Record*, but somehow in the midst of the commitments of writing a weekly column and managing daily life on the farm, the sheer magnitude of the job defeated me. I had done some thinking about the structure of a book, but it didn't start becoming a reality until after I retired from writing the columns and moved from the farm to Fredericton.

I am so grateful for the many people and different skills that came together to help me manoeuvre through the non-writing aspects of creating a book. Our daughter, Hannah Westner, used her networks to find people who could help the project succeed. She also contributed to the editing process along the way. Elizabeth Stockall, the daughter of our parish priest, drew on her editing experience to help us see the vision of how these columns could become a book, helped us establish a process of working together as a team, and eventually researched publishers and happily put us in touch with Chapel Street Editions.

Colin Carle originally came on board as tech support, but has become so much more than that, gently providing excellent editing suggestions (e.g. when he finds a paragraph of more than five lines that is all one sentence), and digging up old (yet new) material for our weekly blog (www.jacoberdman.ca). Our grandson, Stefan Westner, used his skills as a print maker to turn several of Alice's pastel paintings into images that could bring the farm to life in black and white, suitable to this book's format. And finally, I'd be remiss if I didn't mention Sabine Campbell and Kevin Stockall, whose attention to detail in proof reading our draft-material was invaluable.

Lee Whitney
Fredericton, NB
August 2019

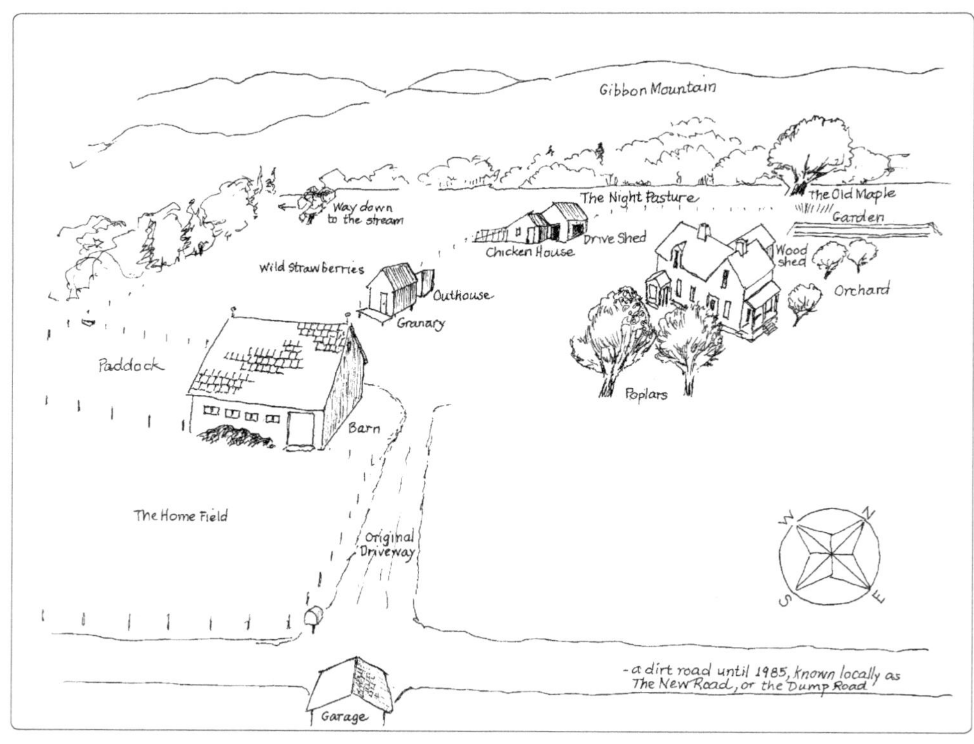

The farm when the Whitneys arrived.

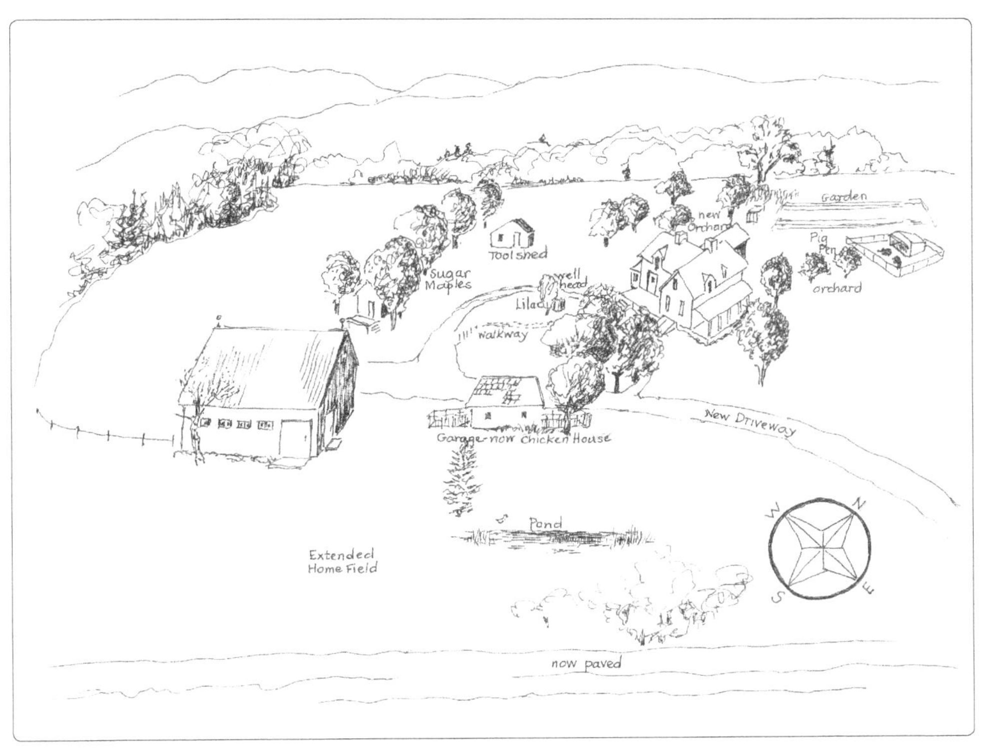

The farm when the Whitneys left.

Notes on the Text

Page Layout

The chapters of *Knowing By Heart* are composed from the author's original essays that appeared as newspaper columns as well as new writing prepared for the publication of the book.

New writing is indicated by regular width margins. The original essays are distinguished by being slightly indented. Flourishes are used to indicate transitions between new writing and the essays and between the essays.

The new writing introduces chapter themes, provides additional context, and creates transitions between essays. Chapters 1 and 2 are composed mostly of new writing, supported by a few excerpts from the essays. Other chapters, except the Postlude, begin with new writing and, in some cases, include passages of new writing between the essays.

Temperature Scale and Distance Measurements

It has long been the author's practice to observe temperature on the Fahrenheit scale and distance in miles. Most instances in this book follow this practice, but a few references to distance in kilometres do show up.

Use of Earth , Nature, and Creation

The word "earth" appears frequently in this book and is used in different ways. It is capitalized when used as the name of the planet. It is not capitalized when used with reference to terrestrial environments, such as landforms, habitats, and the biosphere.

Similarly, "nature" and "creation" are capitalized when referring to the entire realm of life and the planetary setting in which it exists. They are not capitalized when referring to the processes, relationships, landforms, and habitats that make up the terrestrial environment.

"Even the austerity … [of the house] … was a blessing …"

Chapter 1: Prelude

There are great gaps in my information about the Peninsula and many things pertaining to it of which I am completely ignorant. Nevertheless, I know the Peninsula by heart. That's the way I have known it from the first moment when I, a stranger, set foot upon it. That's the only way it can be known—it, or any other place on the face of the globe. No matter how many facts you may gather or how much intelligence you may bring to bear on the study of any locality, unless you know it by heart you'll never know it at all.

Louise Dickinson Rich
from *The Peninsula*

These pieces are a heart's tribute to a place. No map will point to it or take notice of its existence. For the lawyers who drew up the deed, for tax collectors, for Canada Post, what we purchased was a *space* not a *place*—a space between other spaces, filling in a gap in a jigsaw puzzle of property identification numbers and co-ordinates, not a place with slopes and fields and alder patches, a house, barn, and outbuildings, and centuries of history before we came here. This small place of some 70 acres "more-or-less," in southern New Brunswick, in the Maritime Provinces of Canada, was our home for nearly 40 years, and its particularities, which drew us when we first set eyes on it, were filled with wonders. Real places can only be known by heart.

For many of the years we lived at the farm I wrote a weekly column for our local newspaper. Much of the material in the chapters that follow is drawn from those columns. Originally called "A Letter from Home," I thought of the pieces as an appealing alternative to the letters I should have written (but didn't) to those of our children by then away at university. The weekly attempt to chronicle the little events that were the heart of what we called "daily life" became a series of benchmarks or surveyor's stakes to record the contours of that life, its dreaming hills and fertile valleys, icy chasms and swift-flowing streams.

It was nearly 10 years after we came here that Jacob Erdman—my pen name—first came on the scene. I had always been interested in pen names and what they suggested about the writer and his or her context. It seemed to me that writers would appear under a pen name for a common reason, *viz.*, concealment. Originally, I had no intention to write a column for our weekly paper but when I was argued into giving it a try I turned to the writer's friend—a pen name. Several were suggested, but finally I chose a name from my mother's side of the family, "Jacob Erdman."

We had gotten to know the recently arrived editor of the local weekly paper, Ann Farrell, a lively British newspaper person, who needed writers to reduce the strain of writing both the editorials and the entire op-ed page. There were some things that were written in stone of course. Page two carried the court reports (presumably so you'd know who to avoid), the editorials appeared on page four, more general essays appeared on page five (the op-ed page), and Section B carried the local sports news, obituaries, and miscellany.

Ann was not local, and I had marvelled at her ability to sense what was important and should be covered. (The editor after Ann, a young woman also "from away," as the phrase has it, had written an editorial, shortly after her arrival, criticizing the annual Remembrance Day observations downtown and was never heard from again.) Upon complimenting Ann on her ear for news one day, I was met with a remark that took my breath away.

"I think you ought to write a column for the paper." She looked at me.

"No," I said, "I'm not from here."

"Neither am I," she said.

"But I'm an academic. What would readers do with an account of the eleventh century poem on the prophet Daniel?"

And as far as I was concerned that was that—except it wasn't, as far as Ann was concerned.

At the third time of asking, some months later, I gave way.

"OK, Ann," I said, "but nothing will come of this. I'll run out of material before three months are gone."

"Hmm," she replied. And that was that.

The summer before my senior year in college, I had had a job working as a cub reporter for a daily paper in Pennsylvania, "learning the ropes of the newspaper business." My first job was learning to write obituaries. Yes, there is a basic form—or was then. Next, I learned how to write a news story. The important information went in the first paragraph, less important material in the second and increasing triviality from there down. That way the copy editor could cut the story to fit the space without loss of information. This would turn out to be important when I began to submit columns to Ann so many years later.

When we left the city, we had a big house in a good part of town, ate regularly, and were quite comfortable, but according to the proclaimed standards of the city's Social Services we were, as a large family, living below the poverty line. We continued living that paradox for many years thereafter.

This human life is not now, and has never been, what Thomas Hobbes once claimed was the life of early men: "solitary, poor, nasty, brutish, and short." We are the only creatures who can choose the life we lead. We can even choose to behave like beasts. But, that's our choice, not our destiny. Human life is not, finally, a tragedy. It is, as the Italian poet Dante saw so clearly, a (Divine) Comedy, even if this is not always apparent here below.

> Our coming here was a blessing. Often in the city I would come in the door from the University in the evening just as my wife, Alice, was going out the door to a meeting. There was never enough time to talk over the various problems that arose. Here we all had to work together, and everyone had real jobs to do and jobs that had to be done daily, whether it was mucking out the barn or feeding the pigs or picking up eggs or helping in the hayfield or the garden or milking the cow or getting in the firewood for the winter.
>
> Most of what we did here was very small scale. What we had was food that was as free as we could contrive it to be of chemicals and additives. And we had animals

> who, while they had their role in the domestic scheme, were not "steamed up," pushed, regimented, or numbered. They all responded to good care. All of them, right down to the ducks, turned out to have their own personalities, and if they were occasionally infuriating, well, I have my off days too.

We had our share of ups and downs. A few years after we'd moved, we lost all but one of our small herd of cows to a stroke of lightning. That was a dark day! And not only did animal husbandry have its challenges, but bringing up the children we had gathered around us was also challenging, as parenting always is. Francis Bacon, the English philosopher, said "having children is giving hostages to Fortune." He had a point. The storms and stresses of their growing up were real, but the joys were real as well. Despite the struggles, looking back, we remember many good days when it seemed a kindly God, all unawares, had calmed the rough waters of life's tempestuous sea.

Even the austerity of living, for the first few years, in a house with no bathroom, no running water beyond the kitchen sink, no heat but what could be supplied by a couple of wood stoves, no storm windows, no insulation—even that was a blessing. It was a blessing because it allowed us, willy-nilly, to be closer to the great world around us, to experience it directly, and to know its rhythms in a way that no amount of book learning could have supplied. From an industrial standpoint we lived small.

In spite of our odd ways, or maybe because of them, we were continually discovering wonders on the farm, like the way the seasons unfold themselves along the year, or, at another level, the way water will pursue its own agenda in re-arranging a stream-bed across a bit of lowland whether you agree to it or not.

That great saint of the early church, Augustine of Hippo, commenting on the miracle of the changing of water into wine at the marriage feast at Cana, pointed out that we live among daily miracles. "The greater power is in the creation and governance of the heavens and the earth and the fact that rain water is daily changed by means of grapevines into wine and that from a little seed fruits are created. But because these things happen naturally they seem unimportant…"

Eight centuries before Augustine, the author of the Book of Ecclesiastes wrote: "There is nothing new under the sun." It reads like a condemnation, but it is really an affirmation, though perhaps one more apparent in the life of the countryman than in the life of his urban counterpart. Over and over again we are offered the same experience, and the same opportunity to see through that experience to the meaning that lies behind it and informs it, come what may.

> Over and over, spring follows winter. Over and over, morning milking follows evening milking. The sun is up shedding warmth on the lower field. The birds, returning from their winter southern holiday are building nests. The poplars take up the conversations they had to drop last fall. Autumn's "season of mists and mellow fruitfulness," poignantly brief this far north, gives way to October's flash and fire, to be succeeded in turn by the more subtle splendour of November's dark palette.
>
> Even in the sky above us the constellations wheel and change and return again. Glittering Orion, winter's hero, mentioned in the Book of Job, slowly progresses into the west, followed by his faithful dogs, Sirius and Procyon, while Leo, the lion, waking from a winter hibernation, stalks behind them, to be followed in turn by bright Arcturus, the 'watcher of the bear,' in the constellation Boötes. And with the turning of the stars, the seasons come and go with apparent monotonous regularity, as they have ever done, and yet they are never the same.

Within the apparent change is the stillness, which comes from that Source, "with whom is no variableness, neither shadow of turning." There is, indeed, no new thing under the sun. In spite of our age's proud insistence upon being constantly titillated with "some new thing" (already an old habit in the time of St. Paul), in the country it is still possible to realize that what is to be discovered is presented over and over. The veils are very thin. Through them a voice speaks softly but emphatically, "There. Did you see the point that time?"

In the course of a life that has increasingly seemed to be sailing against the wind of the world's wisdom, we have struggled to see as clearly as possible what was before our eyes. Most of the time we found ourselves standing in our own light. Perhaps, once or twice, we did catch glimpses.

To the family of children, homemade and adopted, who clustered about our table at meal times when small, and who are now grown and on their own, I am so grateful for having had their support and help and sense of shared purpose in our unconventional journey. And to, Alice, my wife, I owe most of the stability and sense of order that we came to enjoy despite my tendency to act recklessly as I went in search of the truth beyond any of the images in which the modern world likes to dress it. But for her and her calm grounding in the very soil of being, this often stressful putting forth of tendrils toward the unseen would have been rootless indeed.

> *Here then will we begin the story: only adding thus much to that which hath been said, that it is a foolish thing to make a long prologue, and to be short in the story itself.*
>
> II Maccabees, 2:32

Chapter 2: Early on a Summer Morning

Precious Stones

An emerald is as green as grass,
A ruby red as blood,
A sapphire shines as blue as heaven,
But a flint lies in the mud.
A diamond is a brilliant stone
To catch the world's desire,
An opal holds a rainbow light,
But a flint holds fire.

Christina Rossetti

Early on a summer morning, I stood looking down the fields through the bedroom window at the day already sanctified with birdsong, watching the sun like a giant refreshed with wine rise over Sharp's Hill on the far side of the valley.

The farm is long and narrow, with the house and barn nestled into a slight fold in the rise of land. Behind me, behind the house and the old drive shed and the vegetable garden, stands our big maple tree, overlooking the whole farm as though it were the echo, in a later and lesser time, of the prophet Ezekiel's visionary cedar; "in the shadow of the branches thereof shall they dwell."

Beyond the big maple, the night pasture slopes up and then slips beyond the rise to fall quite steeply into the wooded valley of the small stream that is our boundary (the same stream that was, our first summer here, also our bathtub.) Beyond the stream, Gibbon Mountain (once a real mountain, millions of years ago when huge dragonflies and early reptiles lived here in dense humid equatorial forests of ferns) rises only a few hundred feet and serves as the backdrop to our life here.

Below the house and barn, looking toward the valley in front of me, what we call "the home field" stops at the road. Below the road, our hayfield, bounded on either side by woods, slopes down to the same brook that rises behind the night pasture. The brook holds this place in a long, affectionate S-shaped curve, crossing from right to left at the bottom of the first meadow and then running out of sight past the second meadow, which has largely grown up in alder bushes. Then, in a deepening valley, in pools and shallows, the brook takes its quiet way past the distant third meadow we call Babylon, in tribute to an English field name for "remote land beyond the river" and to the nursery rhyme, "How Many Miles to Babylon?"

How many miles to Babylon?
Four-score and ten.
Can I get there by candle-light?
Yes, and back again.

If your heels are nimble and light
You can get there by candle-light.

Oxford Book of Nursery Rhymes
Iona and Peter Opie

Babylon has remained bare of trees much longer than the other fields because it is a dome of sand left behind at the passing of the glaciers a mere ten thousand years ago.

Curling around the ruins of a huge elm tree, still flourishing when we arrived but which fell victim to Dutch elm disease a few years later, the stream veers off and away from us at the foot of the woods beyond Babylon. Here and there under the trees in that wood we've found mounds of rock, covered with moss and leaves, which indicate that even this distant silent wood was once cleared for cultivation.

As our stream turns quietly to the southeast, not far from the traces of the cellar hole over which the first house on the property was raised (a double house, for two brothers and their families) it passes beyond our land to wander through the woods until it meets the Millstream, some two and a half miles away as the crow flies.

I was looking out over the Millstream valley, as I did most mornings in the summer. Although we couldn't see it because of the intervening woods, we knew where its river was. On a morning like this, when the sun gleamed as if newly burnished in a cloudless sky, we liked to see a cloud below us, over the river. White and compact, it was just beginning to rise off the valley floor as the sun warmed it. In an hour or so it would rise up from the lower field, brush past the house, to become no more than a line of insubstantial mist against the blue sky and then would be gone.

Fog in the valley was a welcome sight, for it betokened a fair day. Or, as an old bit of local weather lore had it, "fog in the holler brings horses to the collar." That fog meant it really was summer, the brief, heartsome summer of this northern country. From a fog in the "holler" it gathers itself into a lumpy white rope of cloud and begins its slow rise toward the sun that disperses it.

We did not always live on the farm. In fact, we never in our wildest dreams could have predicted that this province we had never visited would come to be our home.

"Home." I would be hard put to say which one of the many places my family lived when I was growing up would qualify for that term. Certainly, 440 Salem Drive, outside of Pittsburgh, Pennsylvania was home for ten years, until I went away to college and my father took up a new position in upstate New York. Certainly, we had lived in a number of small towns in southwest Pennsylvania for most of my childhood, and I spent part of each summer with a great aunt and uncle in the Lehigh Valley of southeast Pennsylvania. Which, of all those places, was "home"?

And then, after the rather rootless existence of college life, another aspect of home came into being with marriage and a family. Alice and I never thought of ourselves as very restless people and yet, in the course of twenty-five years of marriage we lived in three places in southeast Virginia, five places in Toronto, and then a small farm in southern New Brunswick, with a year out along the way to live in England.

I suppose something of each of those goes to make up that elusive idea called "home," just as our experience of all the people we have met goes to make up our understanding of that thing called "humanity." Sometimes a moment, or a room, or a tiny event comes flooding back through the gates of memory and makes you realize that part of your life which you had all but forgotten is, in fact, still somehow present, still living on, waiting for the right thing to set it free, to make it dance before you as if the years between had never been.

I was too young to have been directly involved in that terrible struggle called the Second World War, but one fragment of home that comes flooding back to me was of my father, just in from work, with his chair pulled up to the big radio in the living room. The year may have been 1938 or 39. I can still feel a very peaceful and sheltered place, my parents' presence very comforting, and yet, even then, I think I sensed how terribly tenuous, how fragile, all that was.

Many things have faded into memory since those times, many places that one was "never going to forget" have somehow slipped away until they are only shadowy presences at best. "Home is where the heart is," or, as the Pennsylvania Dutch of the Lehigh Valley would say, "Haym is wo die Hotz iss." Are many of those places, shadowy or vivid, present or past, or yet to come any less "where the heart is" than where we find ourselves right now?

Maybe you remember the old riddle that appears in the New Testament as well as in ancient India; the eldest of seven brothers marries a wife but dies without having begotten children. In the ancient way, the next brother then marries the wife so as to raise up children for his brother, but he too dies without issue. In like fashion, the other brothers in turn are married to the wife and all die. The wife herself at last is gathered to her ancestors. The question is given a special twist in the Bible, but the sense is the same wherever the story is told; when the brothers and the wife are miraculously restored to life whose wife is she?

"Home" is as hard to pin down, to extricate from all the experiences one has had in the course of a life, as is the legality of the wife of the seven brothers. And perhaps finally, it is not just many different places that make up our sense of "home." Even for those of us who have lived in one place all our lives, we are, over time, many different people. What meant "home" to us as children may not be the same thing as when we are just starting out in the world or when we come to have children or grandchildren of our own.

Those of us who have never had to suffer the horrors and dislocation of war or natural disaster have been very fortunate indeed. And yet, from talking to people who have lived through such experiences, I know that such things only sharpen that sense of "home." Home is where the heart is—yes—and who can set up barriers to shut in the heart?

Our coming to the farm was an event that in the world's terms was sheer misadventure. But that world's misadventure may be one of the marks of Divine providence. Or it may not. Much that has been claimed for providence is simply self-will decked out in fancy clothing so as to deceive even the claimant. "Look before you leap" may be folk wisdom but it is wisdom still. "Time will tell" likewise carries a warning to be ignored at one's peril. In our case I claim no wisdom, no entitlement, no sense of inevitability before the event. Years after the event, though, all I have is providence to account for our good fortune.

> *All that piece or parcel of land situate in the Parish of Studholm, County of Kings and Province of New Brunswick, described and bounded as follows, viz: Beginning at the southwest angle of lot No. five granted to Isaac Bunnell and running northeasterly fifteen chains to a stake, …the same containing sixty four acres more-or-less.*

So runs "Schedule A" of what the lawyers call an Indenture, "made this 15th day of October in the year One Thousand Nine Hundred and Seventy Five" by means of which and "in consideration of a sum of lawful money of Canada well and truly paid," Alice and I became the owners of a small farm that we had first seen two months before on the evening of what was only our second day ever in New Brunswick.

We had been driving with friends to the local garbage dump when we saw the property for the first time, hardly the beginning one would pick for a momentous event. But momentous events choose their own beginnings, which we can see only after the fact, or else we would know in advance how every story was going to turn out.

We had come from Upper Canada to find out why these friends, who otherwise seemed sensible, had bought a farm in the area the summer before. As we drove past the property, a beautiful sunset backlit the house and barn, and the whole hillside, as well as a "For Sale" sign. We slowed to look at the house nestled into the shoulder of the hill, with its poplars in front, and the small but sturdy barn, its ridge steady and straight with no hint of the sway back that seemed to afflict so many of the small barns we had seen.

We looked away down the valley past the small garage that sat close to the road at the bottom of the driveway, across tidy fields, and the dark greens of the woods. It was a beautiful time of day and a beautiful view. But I think we must have been like explorers coming over a ridge and looking out on country as yet unsung where only later does the expanse, great or small, take on known contours, acquire history and meaning and fit into the fabric of the life around it.

Our family had driven to New Brunswick from Toronto, where we had lived for more than a dozen years. Neither Alice nor I was a city person, but the fact of the matter was we had lived in Toronto almost all of our married life, and it was the only home our children had known.

The next day we went to have a closer look at what was still just a piece of property. By noon, the day after that, the "property" had become a real place that spoke to us, even though we could not yet hear the words clearly. We had made an offer and it had been accepted. As it turned out, it was one of the best decisions we ever made.

That was a Thursday. Saturday morning, we climbed back into the car for the thousand mile journey back to Toronto, hardly realizing that this mad escapade had altered the tenor of our life entirely. We bought the property thinking it would be a summer home, a retreat from our city life in Toronto. After the first summer we realized just how far a thousand miles really is.

We had acquired a house with no indoor plumbing, rudimentary electrical service, and no central heating, as well as a barn, granary, drive shed, chicken coops, outhouse, and two dug wells. But there was much more to it than that. Without knowing it, we had found our home.

"A week in the province and you did what?"

Friends in Toronto were mostly uncomprehending.

In Toronto, I was part of a church Lenten study examining Francis Moore Lappe's *Diet for a Small Planet*, a book which explores the demands that North America makes on the world food supply, to the detriment of ordinary people in other parts of the world.

We seemed to learn a lot of facts and figures about the situation, but as time went by it occurred to me that, although we were now well informed, this was where the discussion ended. We never quite got to ways we as individuals could lessen the imbalance.

I pointed out that we could all make a beginning by keeping a chicken or two. Waxing enthusiastic, I suggested that not only could the hens provide really fresh eggs for the delight of the family, they would also be free to pick up bugs and slugs that would otherwise be a problem for gardeners. Thinking of our attempt to grow a small backyard vegetable garden, which produced carrots the size of radishes, I also offered that the manure would increase the fertility of the soil. And we would have healthy vegetables that had not been grown on land owned by large businesses that had pushed the small landholders off their property in order to sell to large supermarkets.

The response did not quite match my expectations. As the returns came in, certain words kept recurring, like "dirty," "smelly," "noisy." Some participants who went as far as to say the idea was OK, were also clear that the neighbours would not agree. The evening ended with a general conversation which steered quite clear of any idea of chickens in the backyard. I don't remember that we got any further with the Lenten study beyond the studying. It did seem clear to me that North Toronto might not be the best place to be if we wished to take a personal initiative for our health and for the good of others beside ourselves.

The wife of a colleague, whose family was from Gagetown, New Brunswick helped to put the whole thing in focus at, least as far as Toronto was concerned.

"It's a pity you bought on the wrong side of the St. John River," she said.

Later, when our ground shook and we heard rumbles as of distant thunder from the cannon fire at Canadian Forces Base Gagetown, eighty kilometers away, I reflected that wrong and right, short of the heavenly kingdom, may be subject to interpretation.

There are people who have a great gift for being certain about things. My colleague's wife was certain about which was the wrong and which was the right side of the river. Other friends have been certain about all kinds of other things, from the right way to bring up children to where truth was to be found. We bought the property not knowing for sure what we were setting in train. Only by degrees did we discover meaning in what seemed just an impulse. Somehow, I like it better that way. A good story always has some mystery in it.

This experience taught us why property is called "real" estate. We purchased the farm, using what was left of a small inheritance after a so-called financial planner had made an anthill out of a molehill while assuring us that the molehill would almost miraculously become a mountain.

Put a bunch of dollars out to flourish in what is called "the market" and you may very well wonder where they all got to because they certainly didn't call to tell you they were leaving. Put the same dollars in exchange for a piece of land or a bit of property (you pays your money and takes your choice) and they go to other human beings. Now, however, you can at least grow carrots on the remainder and improve your night vision, something impossible to do on stock certificates.

After all the legal minutiae had been attended to and our rash decision was made, like the cast of Caesar's die, there yet remained a symbolic step. The new owner of a property must "take possession" of his purchase. For us, the action was a memorable one, involving as it did a journey of two thousand miles at the waning of the year.

When the lawyers had finished doing "whereas" and "parties of the second part" it was nearly the end of October. Schools were in full swing, I was in the midst of first term at the college, and we were involved in all the myriad of activities a big city uses to keep its citizens from imagining how happy they could be elsewhere. Even so, it seemed only right that we should do what all the cottage owners of our acquaintance always did at the end of the season—"close up the place."

And so, on a day toward the middle of November of the year 1977 (as all good tales of adventure start), Alice and I clambered aboard our big van, bringing a friend to help with the driving and our oldest daughter, who had not been with us in the summer, and set out to drive the thousand miles and back on a self-declared long weekend.

What is there to say about the drive; it was long, and by the time we were in Woodstock it was already dusk. We couldn't remember the turn-off that would take us to "our" farm so we called the former owners, Burton and Violet Keirstead, who were now living in Sussex. They not only gave us directions, but also offered us sleeping accommodations that night, an offer we gladly accepted. It was the beginning of a warm relationship, one that persisted over the years, which pleased us very much.

Saturday morning was sunny and warm with that slightly fey, hide-and-seek quality such weather has at that time of year, this far from the equator. The trees had all dropped their leaves, of course, and the windows were blank as we approached the house by way of the old driveway, straight up the hill from the road.

We had observed our wedding anniversary during our drive, little realizing that we were about to open a whole new chapter of the family saga. Now the autumnal scene, the white house with its startling turquoise doors, the straight-roofed barn, the fields around about, the valley in front of us, all spoke of the history of another family, one that had lived there for over a hundred years, and we hoped we would be able to keep something of that history intact.

It's hard to account for the feelings one has about places. I remember once in Scotland, driving on a road we weren't sure was the one we should be on. As we drove along, hoping for an indication of our route, we entered a valley, seemingly like any other valley, except this one for some reason made my skin crawl. There was something ominous about it. We found out later we had driven through Glen Coe, site of a dreadful massacre in the seventeenth century. Our farm, however, even in that brief glimpse of a bit more than 24 hours in the middle of November, felt right, felt like a good place; felt like a place, as Alice said at the time, "to live out one's life."

The next summer we returned, and were able to stay for a whole year, thanks to a sabbatical leave from my job at the University of Toronto. We arrived in July, not knowing that we would choose to never leave.

Much changed over the time we lived at the farm. The driveway no longer went straight up the hill, a big elm beside the house died, and the house itself changed more than just its colours. On the kitchen wall, under the barometer, we kept a picture of the way the house looked when we first arrived. For all the changes, though, the house remained what it was—a home, and a good one.

Without knowing what we were doing, we had opened ourselves to learn some lessons that life in the "modern world," generally, was not prepared to teach. Without knowing what we had set in train, we were to discover that living without the shelter of modern conveniences opened our eyes to more permanent wonders. Although we, parents and children, had come with the usual diversity of agendas, something in the new life spoke to each of us. In a world full of things, one occasionally glimpses a truth only fleetingly seen down the corridors of time; not to be possessed by things may be the greatest treasure of all.

Although our eldest daughter still declares, in mock seriousness, that we waited until she had gone to college to put a bathroom in the house, the fact is we came straight from the city and city conveniences, to a country place with the rustic appurtenances of summer cottages we had loved. We lived there for four years before we had the wherewithal to begin thinking about making changes. And if there were complaints (I'm sure there were even if I don't remember them at this distance), they were of the sort that can be summed up under the heading of, "Yes, indeed, it is a fallen universe."

At the end of the sabbatical, I took a leave of absence from the University for another year, still expecting to eventually return. In a way, we were just "camping out" for rather longer than usual. There came a time though, in that second winter, when I could no longer put off making my final intentions known to the university. Following many discussions about the question, Alice and I gathered the children for a family council. The room in which we sat, as I remember it, was rather dark, perhaps a reflection of my anxieties about the impending decision; either we would return to the city and a secure job, house, and friends, or stay where we were and take our chances.

Although at one level there was no question but that we would return, at a deeper level it seemed a tide was running in the opposite direction. I am still aware of the strength of that tide as it appeared in the gloom of that dark evening. None of us, it seemed, were longing to go back to the city, and the "sense of the meeting" (as Quakers say) was positive, not negative. I had worried that this idea of staying was something I was imposing on the rest of the family, but to my surprise, when the question was put, no one wanted to go back. That is one meeting I will never forget.

And so, the unimaginable letter of resignation was to be written and sent off. I fervently hoped that the running tide would not sweep us away into the pathless ocean, to be lost in its dark depths. I also vividly remember, and always will, the day I cashed the last paycheck from the university. We had six children to feed. What were we thinking? But we had some money saved, and we had a house back in the city that could be sold. We could last for a while and explore the possibilities. And so we did, and, as I have said many times, we never missed a meal in all the ensuing years.

No one opposed the plan to stay, despite the lack of modern conveniences such as indoor plumbing, hot water on demand, or reliable electricity. We would eventually address these "shortcomings" and put a bathroom in when there was a room available for the putting. The outhouse still is available, although its principal use now is as a support for a vibrant yellow clematis.

Our great and luxurious outhouse innovation (which I'm sure we read about somewhere, probably in *Mother Earth News*) was the installation of a Styrofoam seat for winter. A visitor in those early days came back from the outhouse with a smile from ear to ear. He had grown up in Wales where the seats, as he vividly recalled, were icy cold slate.

For the modern world, the outhouse is an object of ridicule. A standard item in country gift shops of my childhood was a slim volume entitled *How to Draw Outhouses*—the *reductio ad absurdum* of books that tell the seeker how to draw flowers, trees, country cottages or what-have-you. Nevertheless, I often think of our forays into a bitter winter night just before going to bed and the wonders, like northern lights, that we no longer see because we no longer make that journey.

It was on such a quest, one snapping cold night, as I was waiting my turn outside, that I saw the stars dancing. I had always assumed that the phrase referred simply to the twinkling of starlight in a clear sky, but I know now, thanks to that humble trip across the yard, that there can be some disturbances in the atmosphere that do indeed make the stars appear to jump around as if they were dancing.

The alchemical philosophers were right when they said that the philosopher's stone, which changes base metal into gold, is so common it's thrown in the gutter every day—and, I might add, every night as well if our apparent worldly riches keep us from seeing what is truly to be seen.

One of our discoveries, as we took up our life here, involved the huge sugar maple behind the house and above the garden. It was a tree doubly spectacular because it stood on the top of a rise, which fell away into the valley where our stream flowed. Its yellow-gold leaves in the fall made a spot of colour that was visible from across the valley (some three miles as the crow flies) against Gibbon Mountain's evergreens.

The tree surveyed the whole of the property. It seemed, in some curious way, despite its location at the upper end of the farm, to be the centre around which our life revolved. But, like that eternal point where all our life's lines begin and end, the centre is not easy to find, unless you know where to look.

Years ago, when we first drove past this place, the late August sun was just sinking toward Gibbon Mountain and the long rays of evening light brushed a wash of colour across the big maple tree's leaves. The house, nestled by its builders against the north wind, stood with its back to the protective curve of the hill. The poplar trees at the front corner were in silhouette against the sky. It was just a passing impression, a momentary glimpse, but it has remained with me, reminding me of something Arthur Ransome, the English writer and traveller, said of his beloved Lake District; "No matter where I was, wandering about the world, I used at night to look for the north star and, in my mind's eye, could see the beloved skyline of great hills beneath it."

Many a time since that first evening, when, in later years, gathering hay in the field below the road or just walking through the back of the farm, we have looked up the hill toward the house and the big maple's presence. Depending on where we were at the time, the house may or may not have been visible, sheltered as it is by the three poplars that guard us in the summer from the road and in the winter make a fine tuning fork for the wind to strike. But the big maple was always there, situated as it is just

"The big maple was truly the centre, the still point, of our turning world."

where the flow of our hillside levels out and the domestic yard, outbuildings, and gardens give way to pasture and woods.

It was only in the luminous darkness of the country nights, with that sparkling dust of stars burning holes in the velvet black, that we began to orient ourselves aright. We began to know what was up—literally; to raise our eyes beyond the level of one waiting to see when the traffic light will turn green, to become aware of the constellations as presences, which one could only do in the city by visiting the planetarium.

I suppose I am not the only one who grew up knowing out of all that tapestry of light, only the name and general look of the Big Dipper. From visits to the Buhl Planetarium in Pittsburgh as a kid, I knew that the two stars in the front of the bowl of the Big Dipper could be used to trace a line to the North Star. During our years in the city, even to do that was a challenge because the city is never dark, and the Pole Star is easily obscured.

On the farm, I began to look for the Dipper of an evening and watch its slow turning in the sky. Again and again, I would trace the line out and up from the bowl to the North Star, the star that never moves, the Pole Star around which all the heavens and Earth itself appear to turn. And gradually, as I stood in the darkened dooryard, I could see the darker shape of that grand maple against the night directly below the North Star, spreading its branches into the sky.

A true centre is not necessarily where a survey stake would mark it. The big maple was truly the centre, the still point, of our turning world.

Although much of the farm was treed with species native to the Acadian forest zone (spruce, balsam fir, maple, and birch), species introduced by human settlement grew closer to the house. Out beyond the woodshed was the apple orchard and between the house and the barn there were, when we arrived, big poplar trees. Among them was an elm that had a story to tell, a story that Dutch elm beetles would put to rest shortly after our arrival.

The clump of poplars just to the right of the front porch included an elm tree. Somewhere down among the roots of the elm tree, we were told, was a bottle. In the bottle, on a slip of paper, was written a girl's name, a girl who had not waited for a young man who loved her to return from summer employment on the prairies. The bottle was buried and the tree planted over it. The tree grew and flourished as the seasons changed and the years passed by.

Country life, like the tree, draws its nourishment from the soil and the sky. Like the trees, life has its seasons, and the seasons, while never the same, still have their own profound patterns that return in countless variations as in those anonymous treasures we call folk songs. The older I get the more those old songs, simple and unadorned as they are, speak of the ancient patterns of life lived close to the earth, life with its joys but also with its trace of underlying sorrow. In the old song, it is a briar-rose that grows from the grave of hard-hearted Barb'ry Allen, and as long ago as Chaucer's day the "vine-prop elm tree" was a symbol of true love.

Although an elm seemed rather out of place among those poplars, this particular elm, and its memorial to a lost love, seemed to fit right in. Alas, the elm soon died from Dutch elm disease. There was nothing we could do; the disease felled many a noble tree. All the same, we couldn't help wondering whether the change in the ownership of this place had perhaps broken the spell.

Chapter 3: Ducks, Limited and Un...

From troubles of the world I turn to ducks.

Frederick William Harvey
from the poem, "Ducks"

Somewhere I once read a brief notice about the Ig-Nobel Awards. These awards celebrate the sort of over-elaborate schemes Mark Twain once dismissed as being "like shooting ants with a cannon." For instance, one research project perfected a method of recovering whale snot with the use of a remote-controlled helicopter. Another project determined that cows who had names gave more milk than cows who were nameless.

When we purchased our first cow several people advised us not to name our animals. As I recall, we were told children would react badly if a cow with a name turned up, at least in part, as the main course on the dinner table. As all of the family helped out in one way or another with the creatures that we gathered around us, the advice seemed good. But in fact, our first Jersey cow arrived with a name, "Brownie," and the trend was set. As it turned out, the only person who ever objected strongly to knowing the name of the steak on the table was a new son-in-law, a city lad. I think he still recalls the experience.

Generally, the cows and pigs regularly received names, and some of the smaller creatures won names by virtue of their personalities. All the barn cats had names, for example, but they were rather a special case since every one of them was a distinct personality; the fellow who dismissed some impossible task as "like trying to herd cats" had a point.

I doubt whether the findings about naming cows that earned the Ig-Nobel award have advanced agricultural science materially. But names do help to remember the characters on the farm, and some of our favourite characters were often to be found among the ducks!

I think Walter, our first duck, set some sort of standard for the ducks that followed him. Walter grew to duckhood in spite of difficulties. His very birth seemed a triumph over adversity. I don't remember what happened to his mother. I do remember that we gave a duck egg to a broody hen without much hope that anything would come of the transfer. In fact, Walter's surrogate mother hatched him and, like the proverbial hen with one chick, thought her boy the most wonderful in the entire world.

The trouble started when mother took her chick-duck for a walk down our front field and Walter spotted the pond. Cries of woe and disaster from mother reached the house when her child set forth upon the deep, as no chicken ever had. Her frantic cries brought us running, assuming that a fox or weasel had embarked on a campaign of death and destruction. Alas we had no way of explaining her problem to her, and Walter didn't seem to recognise his mother's concern.

In most ways, though, Walter was a dutiful son. He knew about water and approved of it, even if mum didn't, but he was a firm believer in the buddy system and would only launch out on the deep if there was somebody standing by to rescue him should a storm arise. Frequently, it was one of the children who went with him and served as lifeguard.

One day, returning from the pond he met a pony we were boarding. The pony wanted to play, and broke Walter's leg, which we bound up with Popsicle sticks and adhesive tape. The leg healed satisfactorily but ever after (so Alice claimed) Walter had a limp. She could distinguish Walter from the group of other white ducks we kept for several years. How, considering that all ducks waddle like so many sailors on shore leave, would one know? There were moments though, when Walter's identity was clear.

Walter was odd, even for a duck. For one thing, he was never quite sure whether he was a duck or a chicken. When he was a bit older, he would travel with the other ducks but, every once in a while, it would come to him that he was every hen's image of a real hunk.

Poor Walter. Head down and travelling fast, he would pursue the hen of his dreams—she squawking loudly—across the yard. Object: matrimony. Result: rejection. Walter would wander off looking bemused and return to the flock of ducks.

Speaking of ducks, ours have had some trying times recently. There was the morning a while back when the sun's reflection in the pond did not waver but stayed oh-so-still. It's bound to happen at some point every fall, but the moment when the pond freezes over and stays that way until the next spring has a poignancy about it. The ducks had been swimming in ever-decreasing concentric circles for some days, but one night the temperature fell a couple of clapboards below freezing, and the next morning there was no open water at all.

In the summer, the ducks stay out all the time and are quite content to camp by the pond. Come fall, though, they have to be put in at night or during bad weather, otherwise they come and complain under our window. The big box stall in the barn worked fairly well last year as a duck pen, and this summer we tucked them in there every evening and slept the sleep of those who have stashed their ducks out of earshot.

Every evening, there they are, waiting to be let in. Of course, the horses have to come in first, as befits their superior breeding and their high impression of their own worth. Then come the cows—plod, plod, plod. The ducks never seemed to get the seniority straight. The horses would march in through the turmoil of ducks, but no duck ever perished in the rush. I think it's the clearest evidence for the existence of God. Somebody had to be looking out for them.

Often, there was drama; would our heifer, Lucy, be able to psych herself up to step across the barn floor gutter?

Or will this be one of those heigh-diddle-diddle times when she decides to take to the air to avoid whatever it is she thinks lurks down there? The whole manoeuvre is heart stopping. You wish she would finally figure out that whatever it is she thinks she is avoiding is the merest nothing compared to the possible consequences of her aerial displays. Finally, however, Lucy and the dust settle, the stanchions are all shut, and that comforting sound of munching fills the air with a sense of peace.

But wait. While Lucy was defying all of Newton's hard-won laws of physics, reality had, as it were, vanished away. Now, reality begins to reassert itself. There is no sound of peaceful munching to be heard. Not because it is not there—you can see the slow jaws moving, all right—but a wild chorus of quackings makes it clear the ducks are here as well, piled up in front of the closed door to the box stall. They cannot imagine where their pen has gone, they are certain it was right here this morning, yes this is the spot, the grain is missing, why aren't we eating, this is terrible, what is happening to us, oh dear, oh dear, what will we do, my dear, I've never seen anything like this in all my days, where has our pen gone - and so on, and on.

Through it all, absolutely no vestige of genuine thought can be perceived. Only a sort of jamming of the airwaves that continues, deafeningly, until you reach over and open the door to the box stall and they all rush in, heedless of their perplexity of the moment before, but still in a dither because of course this is their pen, and the grain is right there, etc.

This scenario is repeated in reverse the next morning, when the weather is good enough for them to go out. One is greeted, upon arrival at the barn, by the deep nickering of the horses, the crash of the stanchions as the cows heave themselves to their feet, and honks and quackings from the ducks who cannot think why they are not at the pond, where are they, what is happening to them, and so on. When you open the door of the box stall (heaven help you if you have forgotten to open the door out of the barn first), they are off and running for the pond, and peace and quiet reassert themselves on the barn floor.

Three days after the really cold weather began a few weeks ago, we knew we had a problem. The name of the problem was Sir Francis Drake. Interested in history as we are, it is hardly surprising that somewhere along the line one of the male ducks would acquire this inevitable appellation.

Our Sir Francis—to distinguish him from his namesake who insisted on finishing a game of bowls before going to finish off the Spanish Armada—is not like other ducks. At least he is not like any other duck we have had. For one thing, all the other ducks and drakes have been dim-witted to the last degree. They had their mouths open all the time. The vapidity of their conversation had to be heard to be believed. Sir Francis, on the other hand, is a duck of few words, relatively speaking. For another thing, all the other ducks have been white. Sir Francis is largely black with some white markings. But the thing that really sets Sir Francis off from the rabble is his walk.

When parading through the yard, all our white ducks looked like sailors just back to land from a three year's cruise; they rolled when they walked. Sir Francis never waddles. How he does it we are not sure, but however it is, the feet go around just like any other duck while the duck above the feet glides onward like a big old Buick on a smooth road.

Last fall, Sir Francis was our only duck. As the days got colder, he continued to make his dignified way up from the pond every day for a bite or two of grain but always returned to the pond. There he would float, like some old gent at his club, and every day there was more ice on the pond.

After three days of bitter cold we woke to find Sir Francis up on the ice. His water had disappeared, but miraculously he was still alive. There was nothing for it but to go down to the pond and plot stratagems and wiles for arresting the truant but unrepentant duck.

My dearly beloved kindly allowed me to go out on the ice in the hopes of a snatch and grab. Sir Francis was having none of it and I rashly attempted to pursue him through the cattails as he departed for the far side of the pond. I soon discovered it's really true that wool is warm even when it's wet. Sir F.D. left in a hurry while I went down on hands and knees in a foot of water. Water—super-cooled—poured in through the scuppers, finding a happy home in the wool felt liners, wool socks, mitts, etc.

Having done my bit for the second law of thermodynamics I emerged to find Alice clutching the duck and only mildly interested in what I felt sure were signs of incipient hypothermia.

Sir Francis is now residing alone in the box stall. The felts from my boots dried out nicely after a week under the wood stove, and all is generally well. Oh, by the way, pass me a Kleenex, would you?

Now is the season when all things seem rare and wonderful, when a robin's song strikes the ear as something never heard before, and the merest swelling of the buds on the old lilac is fit subject for conversation as I come back into the still pleasant warmth of the kitchen after the morning milking. Even a seven-day blow of easterly winds seems less vexing than it might at other times of year, especially since the sky has continued to be a blue that can almost be heard as well as seen.

Almost all the snow is gone from the old laneway that leads down to the pond. After their winter in the box stall in the barn we have taken to offering the ducks the opportunity to go out into the big world. Usually they parade out, commenting on the scene, the weather, the colour of the barn door, etc., etc. For a while they would go up to the old chicken house and sit under the trailer that's parked up there, presumably so as to shield themselves from the sun, which wasn't shining but might be sometime.

On a hopeful sort of day, they would find a wheel-rut full of muddy water and spend hours searching it for tadpoles or whatever it is that ducks spend hours searching for in puddles. Of course, they would keep up a running commentary as they searched, but even ducks can't do a whole lot of searching in a puddle. Eventually even ducks get the feeling they have been over this particular patch of water sometime before and lose interest. Then they would go back up under the trailer and be gloomy.

But last week, wonderful to relate, the ducks had a revelation. One little patch of our pond actually thawed out. Well, I tell you, you would have thought they had discovered Lake Superior, they were that delighted. (Alice always strong on fair play, says I would have been pleased too if I had spent the winter in that box stall. She has a point.) The water where the ice had disappeared was maybe two inches deep. The ducks didn't mind. It was real water.

So, the ducks have found spring. I'm sure we'll find it too, if we just keep looking.

Everybody's queer, dear,
Except thee and me, dear -
And even thee's a little queer, dear.

adapted from Sir Robert Owen

Then there's Sir Francis Drake, usually referred to as the Noble Duck. We think the trouble started when Sir Francis' consort, Sue, decided to forgo their pleasant times together on the pond and instead settled down with a little clutch of eggs that she had been putting together. Now, Sir Francis is a duck with standards. Not for nothing is he known as "Sir." Sue, it seems, must be protected.

When Sue first started sitting that summer, she would sit for a little while and then, like a number of ducks we have known, think of several other things she should be doing and go to do them. Sir Francis would always be there to squire Sue around when she left the nest. Even though sometimes in the lonely hours, when Sue was communing with her eggs, he did go down to the pond for a swim, he seemed to have a different view of things than hitherto.

One day he let the dog know that dogs were not welcome at his pond. In fact, Sir Francis seemed to be developing into a real Colonel Blimp, the cartoon character whom *Brewer's Dictionary of Phrase and Fable* describes as "an elderly, unprogressive, reactionary 'gentleman' of somewhat limited intelligence." And dogs were not the only threats to order and stability as far as Sir Francis was concerned.

Francis and Sue had been strolling up from the pond several times a day to scoop up some grain we leave out in a dish for them. After politely showing Sue to the grain dish, Sir Francis would stand well back with an air of *noblesse oblige* while Sue had her tiffin. When she was quite done, he would eat too, and they would then stroll together back down to the pond.

But all that has changed since Sue began sitting. Sir Francis, it seems, has drawn another line. He now takes strong exception to sharing grain with other, presumably lesser, species. He most especially objects to the blackbirds: crows, grackles, etc. This morning I watched him in hot pursuit of a grackle. Sir Francis was making his dignified way up to the dooryard and the grain when suddenly—oh, horrors—he spotted the grackle enjoying what should have been Sue's breakfast. He stopped. He glared. And then… neck out straight, head down, he assumed his "make-the-world-safe-for-Sue" posture and, arrow-like, hurtled forward to meet the enemy.

The object of all this hostility, the grackle of the first part, looked to me like one of those street-smart types who, seeing the rioters rushing in his direction, steps calmly into the nearest doorway, only to go his unruffled way a few moments later after the uproar has passed. Unfortunately for the grackle there was no doorway to step into, and what was approaching was no disorganized rabble, but the avian equivalent of the U.S. Cavalry, coming like the wind and clearly intending to take no prisoners.

Still unwilling to appear to lose his cool, the grackle stepped out of sight around the far side of the wellhead. A moment later, he appeared around the other side advancing in two-footed hops. But Sir Francis was gaining ground.

The grackle, not wishing to forgo breakfast but also obviously wanting to avoid being run over by an enraged duck, hopped around two rose bushes, do-si-doed past the lilac, and, losing ground, headed down the yard. Finally, he got tired of this activity and flew up into a nearby tree, leaving Sir Francis glaring up at him from the ground.

It didn't matter that Sue was not there; he had done his duty. After glaring up into the tree for a while Sir Francis forgot what it was he had come for in the first place and wandered off to see Sue.

It's not easy being a duck, especially a duck with standards.

Remember the ads that used to fill pages of the counter-culture magazines years ago? The sort that began, "Female companion needed for Alaskan life. Must like wilderness, work with equal rewards, and the love of a sincere man." What ever happened to all those yearning people, do you suppose?

I have been wondering about this because we have a duck who should run one of those ads. Sir Francis Drake, the Noble Duck is, I regret to say, a widower.

His widower state came upon him mysteriously last summer when Sue, his faithful wife, disappeared under unexplained circumstances. Some days after Sue began sitting, we noticed that Sir Francis was alone even when he came for grain, and some days after that we decided that maybe a search should be made. No Sue. Whether it was skunk or fox or what we never knew. Sue and her eggs had vanished without a trace.

Francis' lonely state was not too much of a problem during the winter when he somehow got along with the chickens in their new coop. I must confess I worried about him (and, to some extent, the chickens, lest he bully them). After all, ducks like ponds and weeds, not sawdust and dry grain. Now that summer is upon us and the Noble Duck has gone out to spend solitary days and nights at the pond, the situation has reached crisis proportions.

I have to say Sir Francis has changed my mind about the intelligence of ducks. Granted, some of the things he does, looked at casually, do give credence to a low view of duck IQ. But, for example, the last few days he has been spending a lot of time either under or close to our truck, instead of down at the pond. Escaping the heat? Maybe. Then I noticed Sir Francis is spending a lot of time looking at his reflection in the flat, shiny area of the truck's bumper. Not too bright, you say? Well, maybe, but I've seen more than one member of homo sapiens species brought up short by a mirror that happened to be pointing in the right direction.

Watching Sir Francis has given me a new view of the duck's thought processes. "Gentlemanly" describes his treatment of Sue. Granted his view of *noblesse oblige* does not extend to what he plainly would regard, if he had read Kipling, as the "lesser tribes without the law," but I can't be too hard on him there. I've known many an elderly (and not-so-elderly) gent, a model of deportment amongst his friends and relations, whose views on more distant affairs would hardly be acceptable. Sir Francis might not think much of chickens, but at least he didn't insist they all become ducks.

It seems to me even a Noble Duck like Sir Francis goes through life with an unquenchable innocence, not to say naiveté. He admires the truck's bumper because he sees in it the only other duck on the place. Clearly, he thinks that if he is loyal and considerate, the other duck, which he sees in the bumper, will come out and they will be able to go down to the pond together and eat tadpoles.

So, if the *Kings County Record* had a personals column, I think I'd run an ad for him. It would go like this; "Elderly drake, widower of noble character, seeks loyal, motherly duck to share his life. Must enjoy strolling about to see the sights as well as swimming, country living. Object: matrimony. Reply in confidence to…."

"We'll wait up for you. We want to show you an addition to the livestock department." I heard the words with an ominous feeling. We were returning home from a pleasant jaunt down into Fahrenheit country and had called our daughter, who was looking after things at home.

My heart sank at the reference to new livestock. There were two expectant cows in the herd, and our track record of leaving people to look after expectant mothers has not been good. Two years ago, we left a neighbour in charge. We assured her that the cow, who was looking like she had swallowed a barrel and gotten it stuck sideways, was not due to freshen until well after we returned. The calf was born, as near as we could tell, just after we were safely around the corner and out of sight.

This time we had been careful to plan ahead. Both the heifer and the cow were due to freshen but not until the middle of September and this was August. I repeated the conversation to my wife, and we were left speculating. Surely, we couldn't have gotten the dates wrong? Surely, the cow, though fond of early calving, couldn't have been that ambitious? But "an addition to the livestock department," as I say, had an ominous ring to it.

I kept replaying the conversation in my mind. What was the tone of voice in which the words were spoken? Was there just a little edge there, as if to say, "You promised us this would be a simple matter of feed and water, and now look;" I didn't think so, but I couldn't be sure. "An addition to the livestock department" had studied neutrality about it. The words had obviously been chosen with care, a care that was too elaborate to mask some minor event like more kittens.

Oh horrors. More kittens? Surely not! Yet it was true, this had been the year of the kitten. For years the cat population in the barn had remained fairly stable but this year, blessed event followed blessed event with scarcely room to exclaim – or lament – over individual litters, let alone individual kittens.

We had been lucky at giving kittens away, probably because the last great kitten give-away was a number of years behind us, and people had let down their guard somewhat.

Our other strategy was to spay and neuter the cats we kept, but just after spending hard cash to neuter two of the big mommas, Queenie was discovered to have brought forth six more kittens in the seclusion of the far hay mow.

This was a bitter blow. Queenie, easily the handsomest of all the current crowd of cats, was also the one who decided at an early age that people were not to be trusted. Despite all manner of blandishments, she remained aloof, to say the least. Usually she would take one horrified look at an approaching human and scram. Now there were six kittens who had imbibed a deep-seated suspicion of humans with their mother's milk. How would we ever lay hands on them, let alone persuade somebody that one of these obviously hostile balls of fuzz was just the thing they needed to make their home complete?

No, I decided, the addition to the livestock just couldn't be kittens. There had to be some justice in the world. But if it wasn't kittens, what was it?

We arrived home on schedule. Lights were still burning. Our family greeted us warmly (it can't be a calf, I thought with relief) before they said they wanted to show us the new additions. The mystery deepened as they led us, not to the barn, but to the dining room.

There, on a chair, was our big picnic cooler. What was inside? The lid was lifted off and eleven little voices were raised in peeps. We had been made the proud owners of eleven baby ducks. Last year, after Sir Francis lost his wife Sue, a friend took his widowed state to heart and a replacement had been found. Now, "New Sue" had hatched a new bunch of ducklings but decided to leave their upbringing to us. She had returned to the pond and Sir Francis Drake, who was unaware of the blessed event.

Much better than kittens!

About ducks there are a number of things that should be said. We are the owners, if that is the word I want, of eleven ducklings, and I'd like to talk about that.

In the first place, these ducklings do not know they are ours. In fact, if we go anywhere near them (to change their water, for example, or to feed them) they are horrified. A horrified duck of any age is not an edifying sight.

The duck pen has chicken wire around the perimeter, reinforced with one-by-two construction grade spruce. The ducklings, when confronted with a human being, all do their best to wedge themselves in the corner of the pen, so as to hide behind the one-by-two diagonal that happens to be there. Eleven ducklings hiding behind a one-by-two is not a big success. Even if there were just one duckling it would still not be a big success. It is even less of a success since all eleven of them are peeping in frantic tones, lamenting the shortness of life and its fleeting pleasures.

Not only do they peep, they are in constant movement, jostling to be the one duck who thinks it is invisible behind the one-by-two. The result is pandemonium. Any carnivore who happened by would have to have the blind staggers and be totally deaf as well to miss a quick lunch.

Some years ago, we read an article in *Rural Delivery* purporting to give the low-down on the intelligence of the duck. The author had also kept ducks, and, like us, had pondered their ways. He had come to the conclusion that, on a ranked scale, and making due allowances where possible, a duck's intelligence was equivalent to half a spruce tree. Furthermore, a whole spruce tree was a lot smarter than a whole fluster of ducks (which I'm told is not the proper collective noun for ducks, but which seems appropriate to me) because the intelligence of ducks is not cumulative. One duck equals half a spruce tree, but two ducks do not equal a whole spruce tree. Twenty ducks put together still have the native wit of half a spruce tree.

He said (and I have observed the same thing) that if you watch a bunch of ducks going anywhere—watch them closely—you will observe that the ducks in front think they are being chased by the ones behind, while the ones behind think they are following the ones in front. It is a wonder they ever get anywhere. Mind you, I thought New Sue, the mother of this crop of ducklings, showed some native wit in deciding to put this lot up for adoption.

When these ducklings came out of their shells, they wandered off to explore the world, or at least the haymow where they hatched, instead of staying with their mother. Unfortunately, New Sue's chosen nest was amidst a pile of hay bales that had been tossed into the barn helter-skelter. Duckling after duckling fell down the gaps between the bales. At this point, New Sue apparently decided that since her children had disappeared they obviously could look after themselves and returned to the pond, leaving the whole issue of their upbringing to whatever, for a duck, passes for Social Services.

Our daughter and her husband had been alerted by the shrill, but muffled, peepings and had rescued the eleven little fuzz-balls from the hay bales, some of them five levels down. All of them were making a great outcry, which was a good thing because otherwise they would have had very brief lives indeed.

You might think, after their early rescue from a death worse than fate, they would have a degree of affection for the humans who saved them. You might think so. But you would be wrong.

After a short stay in the box in the house, those eleven ducklings were transferred to a spare chicken coop. While the presence of food and water helped them survive, it did nothing for their acculturation, and they remained firm in their belief that any human approaching their pen must necessarily be coming with thoughts of homicide, or whatever the term may be when applied to ducks.

Alice, who continued to look after them in spite of their hysteria, spent weeks trying to convince them that they should go outside and enjoy the fresh air. Alas, the little door, through which grown hens went in and out without a moment's thought, proved to be too much for the mind of a flock of ducks. The problem seemed to be that although they spent most of their time with their bills on the ground in search of goodness knows what, when they moved from one place to another, they stuck their heads up as high as possible, convinced that doom was approaching from every corner. Naturally with their heads held high they could not negotiate an entryway that was wider than it was tall. It never occurred to them to lower their heads even long enough to peek out the opening, to see whether the sky really was falling.

For a long while it seemed we had eleven ducks, growing larger by the day, who not only did not want anything to do with humans, but who did not want to risk an encounter with the rest of the world. Why this should be, was hard to determine. Anyone who has seen the mess made by a flock

"… the ducks became more and more bold about exploring the yard."

of ducks in a small space, splashing in a bucket of water, would flee gladly to the less contaminated out-of-doors. But no; day after day went by and not a duck went outside.

Alice, on several occasions, attempted to herd them through the door. The attempt was doomed to failure; every duck stuck its head up as far as possible so as to see the doom approaching. The whole lot of them ran smack into the wall as if no opening was there.

What could one do? At last, Alice had a brilliant thought. I won't say that she thought like a duck—that would be impossible—but she did think of their priorities and used them to entice the ducklings to come out. One day, instead of putting the water buckets in the pen (they needed two buckets by this time so as to spread devastation over an ever-widening area), she opened the big door and set the buckets right on the threshold.

Waterplay is a priority in duckdom and so, not without alarums and forebodings, mind you, they psyched themselves up to come to the door to splash, although they would retreat in quacking horror as soon as so much as a chickadee flew by minding its own business.

Gradually, over the course of several days, Alice moved the buckets further and further from the door of the pen. After a week of this, the buckets were probably two or three feet out in the yard and the ducks were braving the unknown to splash about.

What a relief it was, that they were no longer making their pen look like urban blight. Furthermore, they were actually poking about in the grass right around the door, as though they might possibly find something of interest there. It was then that I discovered that, of our eleven ducks, five were mirror images of Sir Francis Drake, the Noble Duck, their father, and the other six were spitting images of New Sue, their mother. Was the world ready for another five of Sir Francis? I rather thought not.

A week ago, the breakthrough occurred. After getting further and further out into the yard they apparently spotted the pond and went to investigate. They didn't stay long, and I don't think they got so much as their toes wet, but they did go.

This example of initiative was much applauded by their friends and well-wishers. Our daughter, several days later, having seen no further sign that they were interested in the pond, herded them down there and tried to herd them on to the water. You can lead a horse to water, but you can't make a duck swim if it's afraid to.

We settled back to wait without hope and the ducks became more and more bold about exploring the yard. I was thinking of advertising them as the only known variety of dry-land ducks and making a fortune selling them to museums and zoos, when one morning they all disappeared. That night when I went to shut their pen there were no ducks being horrified. No ducks at all.

The mystery was solved the next morning. There they were, a little flotilla, swimming and diving and generally making a mess of the pond.

I haven't seen Sir Francis yet to ask him what he thinks.

The first ducks we had were all white, and memory suggests there were a lot of them. I remember bringing the old army truck, loaded with hay, up the driveway to get to the barn, but having to proceed at a duck's pace. The ducks, moving in a flock, would never think that if they got off the driveway they might elude the danger of being run over. One had to keep a sharp eye out for the duck who, fearing (I presume) for its life, would stop directly in front of the truck to see how close The End might be. Looking over its shoulder like that, it resembled a crazy white plastic wall clock with the pendulum on the top instead of the bottom. The hot and weary haymakers were always relieved to finally get past the duck blockade.

For a while, we had several male ducks, all of them, like the females, pure white. I had never paid much attention to protocol in the world of ducks, but a family member, visiting one summer, noticed the flock as it travelled, twenty times a day, from the pond where it splashed about up to the dooryard where it would find food and back again. He pointed out that the drakes travelled in a group, looking quite efficient, and promptly named them the Law Firm of Drake, Drake, and Drake. The name stuck but the law firm, as well as its clientele, went into the freezer that fall.

Sir Francis Drake, the Noble Duck, has vanished, and, since he was never one to miss a meal, must be presumed to be dead. His demise brings to an end (for the moment) a long line of drakes who have charmed or amused or infuriated the bystanders on these acres over the last ten years. Sir Francis, may he rest in peace, was yet another example of the endless inventiveness of a kindly, if humorous, Creator. Francis was a remarkable duck. He was, indeed, a Noble Duck, a duck with standards. He is survived by his faithful companion of the last several years, New Sue. He will be missed by all who knew him.

Chapter 4: Joint Tenants with Rights of Survivorship (JTWROS)

The ownership of land in common by several persons where there is a right of survivorship; i.e., where on the death of one joint owner the land as a whole vests in the survivors, and can only be disposed of by will by the last surviving owner. Every joint tenant is seised or possessed of the joint property ... by every part and by the whole. The four unities of joint tenancy which must exist ... are: (1) Possession. Each joint tenant must be entitled to the possession of the whole of the land. (2) Interest. Each joint tenant must have the same estate or interest in the land. (3) Title. Each joint tenant must have the same title; i.e. take in virtue of the same instrument. (4) Time. Each joint tenant must have an estate for the same time.

P.G. Osborn
A Concise Law Dictionary

When living in the country, even in these highly politicized times, the attentive cannot help but be aware that a certain deep joy keeps breaking through, despite difficulties and anxieties; joy, yes, but also humility. It is humbling to recognize that, among the so-called "lower orders" of Creation, virtues like innocence are not entirely lost. Even where we might seem to have set up our standards and pitched our tents, it is also humbling to get some glimpse, through those same lower orders, of our own relative insignificance. We are all, as some legal documents state, Joint Tenants with Rights of Survivorship (JTWROS).

When I was a lad somebody who was said to be "in the bug house" was otherwise known to be more than slightly eccentric. Now that I have reached man's estate the term is more justly applied to this farmhouse I share with a good many four, six, and eight-legged friends.

Sometimes the racket the crickets are making in the living room is such that I can barely follow the baseball game. I ought to threaten them with the less civilized delights of soccer, or even football. And there is a bull cricket somewhere in the kitchen who starts to compose epic poetry whenever someone turns on the kitchen tap. I suppose he thinks the water tinkling in the sink is a rival for the affections of his ladylove. I hate to tell him, but we chucked his ladylove out the door a week ago.

In the city, where we lived for many years more than we intended to, it was possible to regard one's home as one's castle, more-or-less. I say more-or-less because the castle was always under siege of one sort or another. In the spring there were the various tract-carrying and tract-selling religious oddballs who were such a menace just when you felt like doing a bit of weeding in the front flower bed. The tract-bearers would fade from the scene about the time the weeds successfully moved in to take up where they had left off the year before. By then we were faced with the summer influx of screen door and aluminum storm window salesmen.

There were fall and winter sieges too, including the economic hardships created by the oil company and the property tax department. In almost all cases, however, it was possible to identify the attackers as belonging to one's own species. "We be of one blood, ye and I," Mowgli called to Bagheera the panther in Kipling's *Jungle Book*. I could say the same of the tax gatherers and bill purveyors of other sorts that clustered round our door as the seasons came and went. You can't say the same thing to the cricket who is intent on shouting you down in what you had thought was your own living room.

As a matter of fact, though, whose living room is it anyway? This old farmhouse has sat on this hillside for a good deal longer than I have. Barring disaster, it will be here a long time after I am no more than humus. Mice have seen generations come and go sheltered in the comfortable darkness of the walls. If I run a very productive trapline in the fall and winter, it does no more than thin out some of the slower or unluckier among the mousey tribe.

Insofar as we can, we try to share what we have with all the creatures with which we live as "Joint Tenants with Rights of Survivorship." As long as they don't intrude too boldly into our affairs, we try to look after what concerns us, and hope that they will do the same for what concerns them. And we hope that all of us will leave the place a little better than we found it.

Humility is a virtue, and not just for the lower orders. Our new life in the country afforded us ample opportunity to practice it. A theologian once asked the eminent British biologist, J. B. S. Haldane, if he thought any conclusion could be drawn about the nature of God from a study of his works. Haldane is reported to have answered, "An inordinate fondness for beetles." I would add spiders, especially in the spring when the babies emerge from their silken sacs and invade every corner of the house.

Weaving spiders come not here;
Hence, you long-legg'd spinners, hence!
Beetles black, approach not near;
Worm nor snail, do no offence.

Shakespeare,
A Midsummer Night's Dream

I was sitting at my very own dining room table the other evening enjoying a moment's respite from the frenzied pace of the day while perusing the newspaper from back to front as is my wont, when I thought my eyes, never the very best even on good days, were finally giving out; between me and the page I was keenly digesting were spots, spots that kept shifting in and out, up and down in a most disconcerting fashion. Eventually, as I was reading the In Memoriam section, the spots won out in competition for my attention. Nothing I could do—roll my eyes, blink rapidly, tilt my head—would shake the spots. Unlike most of the spots that near sighted people are afflicted with from time to time, these remained in front of me shifting in and out, up and down, a different kind of floater.

Just as I was about to reach for the phone book to look up the hot line for Mental Health, one of the spots slid rapidly toward the table and then applied the brakes, coming to a jerky halt just an inch or so above the surface. It thought better of the descent and retreated upwards a half a foot to consider the next move. I was being terrorized by a bunch of baby spiders letting themselves down by ropes suspended from my ceiling, invading my air space. Not a one of them had so much as a Civil Aviation Authority marker on. At least, I don't think they did. They were so small I couldn't even make out their aviators' jackets, to see whether they really had eight arms.

There are baby spiders everywhere these days. Try as you will, you're bound to tread on one or two in the course of the day without being aware of it. They don't have running lights either. Goodness knows it's not surprising that we're having all this rain, if you believe the old superstition around these parts.

Down in the barn, where the spider population has something worthwhile to work on in the nature of buzzes and creepycrawlies, I haven't seen a single spider of any size, large or small. What is it that spiders do for a living, up here in the house? I don't see what all there is for a young spider on the make to do. A lot of them spend their time in the danker corners of the cellar and I'll bet there hasn't been a fly through those sections oftener than once in the last fifty years.

I've never seen one take an interest in the black beetles that God also seems to find so attractive this time of year (the ones that spend their time materializing in the bottom of the tub or the sink and trying unsuccessfully to crawl out, over and over and over again). What do they do for a living besides sit around of an evening telling tall tales about how they almost succeeded in scaling the west face of the stainless-steel mountain? We fondly nicknamed them "Excelsior" beetles because of their habit of heading doggedly upwards toward who knows what mystic destination, like the hero of Longfellow's eponymous poem.

What are they? Would it help us the least bit if we knew their scientific name? That would only tell us what others like ourselves have thought of them, not what they think of themselves. Where do they come from, if not from the interstices of "our" house? They are not climbing "our" walls, though. They are moving toward a heaven beyond our imagining, following what are, for them, their ancient paths. If we occasionally find their lifeless bodies on the floor of a morning, it doesn't mean they have stupidly mistaken our property for theirs and paid with their life. It may mean that they have found, even in spite of us, the consummation they were seeking since the creation of the world.

Unlike the baby spiders, "Excelsior" beetles come in a somewhat larger size, God apparently inventing them that size and plunking them down in the tub to see whether by any chance this one or that one might have the mother wit to get a running start at the sloping end and so be up and over before gravity caught on to what it was doing. The fact that He keeps trying indicates an optimism of truly extraordinary proportions; especially since—being omniscient—He already knows how all the trials are going to come out. (So do the rest of us, of course, but perhaps it's unkind to say.)

Baby spiders are rather comical, and black beetles do have a naive hopefulness that is faintly appealing, but what

God sees in a June bug is really hard to make out. The idea of animating something that size and encasing it in armour plate and setting it flying to spend its entire conscious life (if June bugs have a conscious life) bashing into your bedroom window or your porch light bespeaks a curious mindset. On the other hand, the June bug might say the same thing about the inventors of plate glass and porch lights.

In our later years in the farmhouse we had fewer opportunities to play host to bats, but in the early days, when the old house was still pretty much as it had been for the past fifty or more years, the occasional bat would creep down from the attic. These midnight flights yielded predictable results, especially after we had put together a bit of money to buy aluminium storm windows and screens. The bats once in, could no longer get out.

It was 4:46 in the morning when a bat appeared for the first time. I know it was 4:46 because I looked at my watch. I bought a digital watch for an absurdly low price several years ago, so I would have something to take with me to the hayfield. If the digital watch died of a surfeit of hayseed I would not even shed a tear, as I would if my faithful, if rather inaccurate pocket turnip were to get crunched. My ten-dollar special not only did not die, it has survived numerous crises and continues to tell time with depressing accuracy. Long after the cognoscenti have discarded digital time, I am still trying to remember whether 4:46 is one minute before or one minute after the quarter hour. Math was never my strong point.

So, when my nearest and dearest gave me a poke in the ribs with her elbow and announced that I was to do something about our little friend, I was able to know exactly when my well-earned rest had been shattered.

There is something about a bat. What it is I don't know, but one's reaction to its fluttering is a trifle cautious. If the guest were a bumblebee, one's approach would be simple and direct. With our bat, though, I found myself ducking involuntarily every time it flapped by.

Of course, I did what any hero of the people would do when confronted at 4:46 in the morning with a summons to "do something about that bat!" I opened the door to our room and politely stood aside. Not being slow of study, the bat, after a zoom or two around the room, was out the door and into the shadows of the hall. Thinking that he or she would be grateful for an opportunity to sample nightlife in the great outdoors, I opened a window in the bathroom and returned to bed, shutting our bedroom door as I went. A moment or so later I was again sleeping the sleep of the just, now with more right, because I had heroically solved a difficult problem.

It was 5:11 when a second poke in the ribs announced that the bat had returned. Clearly, he felt the outdoors was not as appealing as sharing a few precious moments with us. If it is hard to be awakened from a sound sleep at 4:46 a.m. when that sort of thing is not part of your daily routine, it is even worse to be awakened at 5:11 after already having been awakened at 4:46, if you see what I mean.

This time, fortunately, I did not have to work out a new strategy. Avoiding, as best I could, the bat's air-space, particularly after Alice suggested from beneath the bedclothes that rabies might be a reason for Flapsy's presence, I again opened the door and oh so graciously wished it Godspeed.

Again, the bat flew down the hall. It went right past the open bathroom door. I noted that but decided it was just a glitch in its navigation system that the bat would quickly correct. As for me, I again shut the bedroom door and composed myself for slumber. My wife, however, wanted to know how the bat got into our room in the first (and second) place. "Magic," I mumbled, and shut my eyes.

It was not a convincing answer, and my eyes re-opened. A few moments later, at 5:16 to be exact, Alice, in a stage whisper, announced the solution; the dear little thing was back again with us, having crawled under our door to get there. Really. Now, I am all for the wonders of nature, I think bats are fine corporate citizens. No doubt their habits are a marvel to contemplate and worthy of prolonged study. However, I also think a good night's sleep is even more worthy of celebration, and this was not being a good night.

Once again, I crawled out of my warm bed and opened the door. This time I took the precaution of stuffing a towel under the door when I closed it, and so, at last, was able to gather a few moments of sleep in what was left of the night. The fact that there were no blood-curdling shrieks from any of our sleeping youngsters suggests that Flapsy had also had enough for one night.

Where the bat went I don't know. Where do bats go when they are not fluttering about in your bedroom or squeezing under your door? I don't wish to intrude on their privacy and I would hope that they would not wish to intrude further on mine.

On at least one memorable occasion, the bat was the last dramatic straw in a series of last straws on what began as a short night. Some of the house's tenants arrived as part of the family, like the dogs and cats. They added their own drama to our life here, sometimes mixing it up with the original tenants and producing unexpected results.

Although the days have their routines, they vary with the seasons and indeed with the hours and minutes. Once the evening meal is done and chores are over, life settles into a quiet comfortableness.

Tonight, in spite of the mild weather, the cat is in. Both dogs are out. The younger one likes it that way. The older dog guards his comforts jealously and is careful to be inside and inconspicuous by the time I am closing up for the night and shutting off lights.

Occasionally, Baggins, the older dog, finds himself on the wrong side of the kitchen door and does not notice the error until the lower floor is dark. Sometimes I remember to get him in before I go upstairs. But tonight, I look at the outdoor temperature and figure the season has advanced far enough that a night outside will probably be quite pleasant. Before I turn the porch light out, I check to see if he is out there, asleep at the switch. He's not. I make my way upstairs, shutting off lights as I go.

It has been a late night. There has been much to do and the new moon has long since disappeared behind the hill back of the house before we could put out the last light and settle down for a good, if brief, night's sleep.

Moments later, the quiet rural countryside was shattered with volleys of barking as Baggins took violent exception to something and continued to take exception to it all around the house, coming back to the porch occasionally (just below our window) to take further exception before setting off on his vociferous journey once again.

I was not coping well with this activity. A vaguely conscious part of my mind told me I should Do Something, when, to my surprise, Alice, who would speak politely to a riot, was at the window, shouting at the miserable hound to "cease and desist," etc.—not exactly in those words.

Groggy as I was, I was impressed with the fervour of her tone. Baggins was not. After a thoughtful pause to allow us to get almost to sleep, he careened off again in splendid voice calculated to shiver timbers and shatter glass. I reached the kitchen just as he was completing one tour of the house and was returning to the porch beneath our window to report on his progress before setting off again. He was invited in, in no uncertain terms, to spend what was left of the night indoors and I trudged off upstairs in search of at least a little sleep before the day began.

It was probably an hour later when Helen the cat arrived in our room with a thump. We had removed the screens from our bedroom windows for most of the winter. Helen apparently knew this and had gone out on the roof through the open window while we were getting ready for bed.

Helen, whose name was short for Hell-on-Wheels, is not a large cat but she has what might be called a weighty personality. She can make a simple trip down the stairs sound like the footfall of a stampeding rhinoceros. Even so, the thump that announced her arrival was not as interesting to our foggy minds as were the evident sounds of struggle, accompanied by what sounded like flappings. "Oh no, she's got a bat!" was Alice's speedy diagnosis.

I was just getting my faculties reassembled when a Great Awakening with cries and thrashings erupted right beside me on the bed. Helen wished to share her good fortune with us and had brought her bat, still flapping spasmodically, with her as she jumped on the bed, landing heavily on Alice.

By the time I had responded to the Great Awakening and was on my feet, Helen and her trophy had been dumped back on the floor and Alice had taken refuge beneath the bedclothes from whence muffled pleas to "Do Something" continued to surface. After deflecting Helen's attempt to go to ground behind the dresser with her prize, she was eventually invited to enjoy her late-night snack in the remoter corners of the house.

Moments later, or so it seemed, the clock radio weighed in with the grim news that another day had dawned and it was time to rise and shine.

It was a memorable night but we are not anxious to repeat it. Baggins is sleeping inside at least for the time being, and this morning I put the screens back on the bedroom windows.

The barn, where our Jersey cows lived, was a busy place, full of tenants of its own. Growing tired of chasing mice out of the feed bin when I wanted to get grain for the cow, we had got a barn cat. In short order we acquired quite a crew of cats who all regularly showed up at milking time to be given their portion of the wonderful, rich Jersey milk. They were entitled to it, I felt, because mice in the feed bin had become a thing of the past and continued to be conspicuous by their absence as long as we kept a cow.

There were other tenants of course, including the flies that initially I tried to control by commercial means. Although I never used poisons, I did resort once to a giant sticky flypaper only to discover to my horror that it had caught a bat hawking for flies too close to its surface. By the time I made the discovery, the bat was dead.

At that point I turned instead to the resident grey spiders who liked to build webs in the sunny windows and elsewhere. At first, I had tried to tidy them away, but after the flypaper episode I recognised them for the helpful citizens they were. It was only as the weather began to turn cold in the fall that their presence became something of a problem.

> I opened the door to the barn this morning and strolled in only to be practically decapitated by a guy wire strung across the walkway sometime during the night by a determined spider.
>
> I've discovered over the years that being tall has its disadvantages. For example, no matter where you position yourself amongst a group of hikers it will be your privilege to discover more spider webs slung across the path than are discovered by anybody else in the group, with the possible exception of the leader. If you're tall, it's a serious error in judgement to volunteer as leader on a hike. Everybody behind skips along free of anxiety because you get all the spider webs.
>
> This morning, though, being tall had very little to do with the case. In fact, the only way I can get through the barn each morning without being garrotted or otherwise disabled by a spider web, is to get down on my hands and

knees. Even then I bet there is some spider down at ground level just waiting for me to come by.

I don't mind spiders most of the time. They are diligent citizens, doing work I wouldn't care to tackle, for wages I shudder to contemplate. I do rather object, however, when, having unintentionally walked into a web, I later find the owner of the web wandering moodily around my shirt collar looking for a suitable site to begin reconstruction. I wonder what exactly she has been doing all that time before I noticed her and what she might have done if I had inadvertently offered her what she might consider an insult of one sort or another.

The spiders who live in our barn are mostly grey and, this time of year, impressively large. Their webs and the associated guy wires are correspondingly heroic. The Sussex Naturalists Club could probably tell me what kind these spiders are but I don't know that it would help much. I do know that as summer fades away, the spiders begin to get anxious, and an anxious spider is one that wants to make sure she has a web of the very highest quality.

How do you say, "The end of all things is at hand," in spider language? The whisper seems to be shaking the guy wires. Every spider, secretly convinced of her personal immortality, is busy extending her area of operations as rapidly as possible. As you no doubt were told in high school biology, or in some natural science exhibit, or in Ripley's Believe-It-or-Not (if you are as old as I am, which is not likely), the strands of a spider's web are stronger by far than the equivalent thickness of high tensile steel.

Comparing spider webs to steel cables is something scientists do as a way of keeping the grant money coming. They call it "extrapolation," "extrapolate" being a scientific word they like to throw around. If you ask what it means they are likely to use other big words like "parameters" and the next thing you know they are drawing diagrams on the blackboard and talking about the x-axis and the y-axis.

You know the sort of thing I'm talking about. "Did you know," they will say, "that if that ant carrying that insect were as big as you, it would be able to pick up a fully loaded tractor trailer and walk off with it?"

Naturally, they expect the ignorant masses they are addressing will be slack-jawed at this demonstration of the superiority of scientific thinking and will then burst into rapturous applause and renew their grant. Never mind if that ant were as big as you its hard shell would be so dense and heavy it would be lucky if it could wave an antenna before doing an imitation of Humpty Dumpty's misfortune for which he is rightly famous.

I have to admit, though, scientists are on to something when they compare a piece of spider web to a piece of steel wire. I must remember to park a stout cudgel beside the barn door this evening so I can wave it before me tomorrow morning as I attempt to penetrate the interior. Maybe I can convince somebody that the End really is at hand.

As we settled into our country life we began to take a different attitude toward the creatures around us. Like the spiders that I had first regarded as a nuisance and then came to see as helpful, in spite of our occasional conflicts of interest, the wild world around us became more and more a part of our lives and filled with meaning, even if we could not always say what that meaning was.

Old stories of wonders hidden in apparently meaningless events came to mind, as if to remind us of the wonders hidden in the everyday. We were beginning to "touch the earth," not as owners and superiors but as attentive students listening to a wise teacher. Beyond the house and barn, other wildlife also co-habited the farm with us.

After many years of saying to each other, "What bird is that?" we finally purchased a set of tapes guaranteed to make us better listeners to the language of birds.

The ability to understand the language of birds is one of the motifs that shows up regularly in fairy tales and myth, where it usually helps to get the hero out of some tight spots. I can understand why. A lot of what I hear from birds seems distinctly like information. Perhaps that information might tell us behind which of the three doors is the passage leading to the great treasure, or warn us whom to avoid to escape enchantment?

The world looks plain enough to us as we see it, but who knows what enchanted lands might be in front of our uncomprehending eyes? If only we knew which tree was the Eildon Tree under whose shade Thomas the Rhymer rested one summer's day some seven hundred years ago. It was under the Eildon Tree that Thomas met the queen of Elfland:

And see not ye that bonny road,
Which winds about the fernie brae?
That is the road to fair Elfland,
Where you and I this night maun gae.
He has gotten a coat of the elven cloth,
And a pair of shoes of velvet green,
And till seven years were past and gone
True Thomas on Earth was never seen.

Anonymous
The Romance of Thomas of Erceldoune

Shortly after we moved to the farm, a friend and avid birdwatcher and listener came to visit. I don't remember exactly when he was here, other than sometime in the early summer when most of our local birds are busy spreading news of damsels in distress, and dragons hoarding great treasure.

In the course of a short walk one afternoon Jim wrote down the names of all the birds he heard. I still have it. On a day when, if pressed, I would have been willing to swear to a few crows, the occasional robin, and maybe a song sparrow, Jim had heard 51 birds and wondered about 7 more.

His list included the finer details of what I had lumped together under the heading "crows." His list included crows, ravens, starlings, grackles, and cowbirds. It also included the red winged blackbird I had forgotten to hear, and the blue jays that I never seem to hear until the leaves begin to fly in autumn.

He had also heard robins and song sparrows. But he had heard the rose breasted grosbeaks as well, those colourful birds whose long rich song sounds very much like a robin who has taken singing lessons. And he called my attention to the bobolinks. How was it I had never really focussed on bobolinks until Jim came?

One memorable first day of spring, many years ago, I first heard the English skylark while Alice and I were walking along a public footpath in the country not far from Oxford. Now, when the bobolinks come back to the farm and begin to sing their warbling "bobolink-bobolink, spink-spank-spink," it reminds me not only of the sweet countryside around me but of a walk to a holy well one spring day in England.

We have since come to know many of the birds on Jim's list one way or another, although usually by sight rather than sound. Evening grosbeaks, rose breasted grosbeaks, purple finches, chickadees, goldfinches and white-throated sparrows are all familiar visitors at the feeders during the winter. Flickers flicker in and out of the woods this time of year, and the dusk of evening is made magical by the calling of the wood thrush from within the darkening woods around us.

Far in the pillared dark
Thrush music went –
Almost like a call to come in
To the dark and lament.

Robert Frost
from "Come In"

We frequently see hawks floating across the sky, as well. In no danger of being a hawk's dinner, we stand still and watch their soaring grace. Closer to home, but in a way no less distant because of his burning intensity, the hummingbird is even now feeding at the bergamot. Although much less intense, the barn swallows are spectacular avian stunt pilots. They do Immelmann turns and loop-the-loops in the door yard and then suddenly stop to gossip on the telephone wires before frisking off again. Sadly, their numbers are greatly reduced these last several years.

There are more wonders to discover. Several weeks ago in Fundy National Park I saw my first warbler, but I have yet to hear one sing. Jim heard eight different warblers on his visit to our farm. What other songs reach our eardrums but never register? What birds, do you suppose, were singing in the Eildon Tree that summer day so long ago? Can we train our ears to catch the song?

Looking back over your life, can you call to mind a distant place or time now fixed in memory because of some small detail that would probably have been all but unnoticed at the time? Our resident frog chorus was just such a beloved feature of the farm. Spring is an awakening in more ways than one.

In thinking recently about the way the snow receded from the fields and the buds on trees and bushes began to swell and how the water in our pond lost its winter rigor, I can, at least fleetingly, sometimes catch memory at work. There is no question of dictating to memory what it is we should treasure. Age and experience make us chary of thinking, "I'll never forget that as long as I live!"

Part of my memory of spring on this farm is going to be the evening chorus of frogs and peepers that begins when the snow and ice have gone, except deep in the woods and along the shady edges of the fields. They shout their

"…the dogs are asleep…on the porch."

exultant songs of rebirth when, to the rational mind, there is precious little cause for hope. Barnyard, dooryard, and fields beyond are all dull brown in colour. Only the pussy willows at the roadsides are willing to make a cautious move toward celebrating the season to come, but the gang at the pond have thrown caution to the winds.

Our bedroom has windows that look out on three sides: to the hills behind us, to the dooryard and barn, and toward the pond and the fields below the house. Depending on which way the winds are blowing, we can adjust the ventilation, opening the window looking down the fields if the wind is strong from the west, and opening the one looking toward the hills if the east wind seems troublesome. Whatever window is opened, the sounds of jubilation at the pond are sure to come in along with the fresh air.

This year, in spite of what seemed a very persistent east wind that worried the curtains and whistled around the sash, the window toward the pond and the fields below has been open to bring us the high clear treble of the peepers, and the baritone gabble of the wood frogs. I feel about their song this spring as A. E. Houseman felt about the cherry trees "hung with bloom along the bough." Life is short and uncertain, a season as precious as spring should not be squandered as if we would live forever. And even if we could live forever, the mystery of the renewal of life in the spring is always new, always something to attend to, to treasure.

Let the east wind blow. Chickens and ducks are quiet, the dogs are asleep in the kitchen or on the porch. The cows, after their evening ration of hay and grain, are settled in their stanchions. In the peaceful dark as we settle into sleep the joyous song of the frogs calls us to lift up our hearts, to rise above the day's troubles, and to rejoice.

Chapter 5:
Seasons and Ceremonies

I bind unto myself today
The virtues of the starlit heaven,
The glorious sun's life-giving ray,
The whiteness of the moon at even,
The flashing of the lightning free,
The whirling wind's tempestuous shocks,
The stable Earth, the deep salt sea,
Around the old eternal rocks.

Cecil Frances
English Hymnal
From "Saint Patrick's Breast-Plate"

And the spring comes slowly up this way.

S. T. Coleridge
from "Christabel"

After long winters, the snow would begin to melt away into the ground, and our cast-iron rabbit became visible once again. Snowdrops bloomed in the snow and everywhere in the fields green spears of grass thrust themselves through the thatch.

Suddenly, it was hard to stay inside, and the interior door stayed open most of the day. The storm door had more glass and let in more light. It was a different light from the white light of winter and it had a different effect. Winter sunshine often comes with very cold weather and, more often than not, with cold winds as well. The light the sun shed on us during its winter journey across the sky hit at a very low angle, making colours seem more intense than they were in the heat of summer. Separated from the cold air outside, the sunlight provided a surprising amount of warmth in the house for a few hours in the early afternoon. But much sunlight in winter came on the rebound, bouncing off the snow before it came in the windows. The reflected light on the ceiling gave the room a rather cool, clinical quality that reminded me of hospital wards back in the days when it was thought, oddly enough, that lots of sunlight and fresh air was good for everyone, sick or otherwise.

Somehow, I missed the pussy willows this year until after they had turned into fuzzy yellow blobs of pollen. And just yesterday, as I was returning from town, I finally caught a glimpse of the yellow blooms of the coltsfoot at the corner of the driveway, opposite the mailbox. Coltsfoot is sometimes called "son-before-the-father" because the blooms come before the foliage. Alice saw them days ago.

As much as I like Emily Dickinson's poetry, I think I caught her in trouble with a metaphor in a poem I had not noticed before—"Nature Rarer Uses Yellow." I found this poem last evening when I was looking for something else.

Nature rarer uses yellow
Than another hue;
Saves she all of that for sunsets, —
Prodigal of blue,
Spending scarlet like a woman,
Yellow she affords
Only scantily and selectly,
Like a lover's words.

The testimony of the pussy willows and the coltsfoot contradict her. She might argue for the sparseness of the pussy willow but the coltsfoot is hardly sparse. Then there are the dogtooth violets that will soon be blooming along the fence row beyond the orchard—great yellow drifts of them.

And the forsythia out the back kitchen windows is nearly luminous with yellow blossoms up and down its branches. I can't believe Emily wouldn't have known about forsythia. For the first time since we planted it some years ago, the whole bush is ablaze this spring. Whether this is the result of maturity or a winter less difficult than past ones is hard to say. Like the coltsfoot and like the poplars beside the house, the forsythia believes in doing everything at once.

Lilacs are cautious about putting out the tips of young leaves a little further each day and only when they are sure the coast is clear do they begin to think about flowering. Coltsfoot, poplars, and forsythia are of a different temperament. They go for broke, firing off blossoms like dispatches from the front, excitedly issuing bulletins and apparently letting the supply trains catch up with them if they can, rejoicing in the danger and scorning the lilacs' steady but cautious advance.

What about the clematis? The good, old-fashioned purple one we planted beside the kitchen porch tried life for several years and decided not to take up the option. Across the dooryard, however, a yellow clematis is ecstatically happy where we planted it to disguise the outhouse, which was the sum of the "facilities" for the first few years we lived here. Whether the purple one found living next to a downspout from the rain gutter too much of a good thing, or whether the resident wild rose bush was scornful of the newcomer, we will never know, but its yellow cousin across the yard is doing marvellously.

And hey, Emily, did you forget about the dandelions? I know people get edgy about dandelions, but really, they are a sight for sore eyes after a long winter. We are calmer about the coltsfoot and the forsythia and the clematis and the dogtooth violets and are willing to be content with admiring them. After all, they're not going to try to take over our personal space. But really, it must be a very hard heart indeed that can't admit, however grudgingly, that in full bloom the dandelions really are quite splendid.

No, I don't think this idea that all nature's yellow gets dumped into sunsets will stand examination. But wait, there's more. What about daffodils? What about buttercups? What about goldfinches? As for sunsets, the only yellow ones I can remember appeared over tidewater Virginia many years ago when we lived there. The yellow effect was rapidly followed by skies of an unpleasant green, and those in turn were followed by a hurricane. Hardly "lover's words."

I rest my case. I may not see things that other folk see quite plainly, but I can spot a poet in trouble with a metaphor when I see one.

I remember how each spring on the farm the green began to show among the brown grass on the sunny slope and how the snow retreated into the shade of the woods; that's when the crocuses came up against the basement wall. As warm days succeeded cool nights, the sugar maples along the fence row beyond the orchard were tapped and another important spring milestones was underway—the maple syrup season.

We passed several seasonal milestones a week or so ago, and I just want to go on record as saying it's fine by me.

The lilacs on this place have been watching the weather for a lot longer than I have. Some of them, I suspect, have had an interest in things on this hillside since Queen Victoria's time. I've never checked to see if they respond to "God Save the Queen" or are particularly perky on what used to be Victoria Day. A good deal of what else is here on this homestead has been here that long or longer, and these bushes don't have the look of upstarts.

Now that the frost is out of the ground and we haven't had a blizzard for a couple of weeks, we can rest our eyes on the lilacs and observe that the first leaves have emerged. Once they are the size of a mouse's ear we know we can put the onions and the lettuces in the garden, as well as other garden crops that don't mind putting up with what could best be called "adverse conditions." If our lilacs commit themselves to leaves, the chances are pretty good that cold season crops will do all right too.

Other signs of advancing spring have now appeared as well. The first backhoe of the season came up the drive the other day. I don't know why it is that your yellow-beaked backhoe is so attracted to this hillside but every year around this time we can expect to see one (we've never actually seen a pair) in the yard somewhere, rooting around in search of something. In fact, we encourage their presence. The one that showed up this morning, for example, set in to rooting up the foundations at the near end of the barn, and before you could say Jack Robinson the ground was ready for a cement barricade, which should put a stop to the seemingly endless reruns of Noah's Flood in the barn.

There is much to be said for the old style of barn building. I have always suspected that a barn like ours could be tilted over on its side and put back again without deforming, assuming you had the levers with which to do it. Now, I'm sure. Here was our barn, suspended in mid-air all along one side, without the slightest sign of discomfort. All the same, it was a rather alarming sight.

There was really no foundation under the barn to root up; only some rocks that looked as though they were seeds for something like Mount Everest. Below that, what I thought was a ledge of rock turned out just to be winter still hanging on. Here, down in the still frozen earth, there was a bubbling spring. Maybe the reason we have so much trouble with water here is that this is the site of an old ocean and it hasn't finished draining yet.

One way and another, the spring milestones are flashing by.

Years ago, when we were new on the farm, the blooming of the poplars had the quality of magic. In what seemed like a single day, bare branches that had been visible since fall suddenly darkened the sky with thousands of long drooping catkins. How could it be possible for trees to do that in the few hours between the end of one day and the beginning of the next? I would tell myself that next year I would pay attention. And of course, when next year came around I would realise—too late—that I had forgotten to pay attention again.

Gradually, though, we learned habits of watchfulness that had been quite unnecessary in the urban world we had left behind. In the city, the great world of sky and cloud, death and rebirth of growing things, drift of stars, and moving planets hardly registered. Almost from our first day on the farm, I kept a daily weather journal recording temperature, barometric pressure, frost dates, rainfall, snowfall, and what we observed in the sky. This discipline over almost forty years helped us become more observant.

> Earth, air, fire, water; everywhere we turn on the farm something momentous stirs us, and the change of pace leaves us wondering. Our tiny corner of the great world renews itself before our eyes and yet we never quite succeed in catching nature in the act.
>
> We went to bed one night a while back, looking at a world still inclined to browns and greys. The next morning, I noticed the big white poplars by the front of the house were entirely hung with their caterpillar-like flower clusters.
>
> How had all those flowers got there? In a good deal less than ten hours those trees had decided that the time had come to bloom and had manufactured the whole apparatus out of nothing. Who says trees are a slow study?
>
> Even the clouds change their shapes as this season advances. Winter's clouds are dark, and we've had our share of dark days this spring. The clouds that laze about overhead these days, when they aren't ganging up on each other, or on us, are chubbier and more relaxed-looking than their January cousins.
>
> Except for the hardy types, who seem to go around in shirtsleeves in weather that still has me looking in the bottom drawer for the long underwear, the temperature

is not yet exactly hot; but those clouds now up there look like they know what warm weather is and swell with incipient nativity.

Have you ever thought about clouds and how they inform our whole view of, not just the sky, but of our very existence? We talk about "a cloud on the horizon" when we mean that something in the future is worrying us. "Storm clouds" can be anything from the build-up to a world war to the domestic consequences of overlooking an anniversary. In the latter case, the storm clouds may no longer be on the horizon; they are more likely to be overhead and we speak of ourselves, ruefully no doubt, as "being under a cloud." Clouds can have "silver linings." Some of us may travel around with our "heads in the clouds" (none of present company, I'm sure). And those who have their "heads in the clouds" may come up with "cloud palaces built in cloud-cuckoo land." However it is, the clouds these days seem just as pregnant with new life as the earth itself.

A few days after the poplars surprised us with their impetuous fertility, I took courage in both hands—it being a damply dark day with no hint of wind—and burned off part of the field around the garden perimeter.

Owing to the slope of the surrounding land it is almost impossible to mow the edge of our garden patch. Over the past several years I have plotted various stratagems to combat the encroaching wild, but every year the wild sneaks up on the tame and menaces the polite little lettuces and peas, marching along in their well-organized rows.

With a pocket full of matches and an old broom, I set out to get rid of, at the very least, the thatch that had built up. "Playing with fire" is widely regarded as a foolish exercise. I must say I was glad the air was damp and windless as the flames, in the Psalmist's words, "licked up the stubble." A few hours later there was nothing to be seen but the black residue of a fiery consummation. By then, the wind was picking up, and a bit of a breeze suddenly showed fiery teeth that ran snapping through a mouse nest and some thick thatch with an obvious appetite for bigger things.

But the breeze dropped, and before it gathered its breath again my broom had quelled the fire from an incipient love affair with the field at large. Water followed fire, water in the form of a soft rain that night. The blackened desolation softened almost overnight into new green.

Earth, air, fire, water; the four great building blocks, all are bound into a burgeoning of new life this time of year.

O, to feel the beat of the rain, and the homely smell of the earth,
Is a tune for the blood to jig to, and joy past power of words;
And the blessed green comely meadows are all a-ripple with mirth
At the noise of the lambs at play and the dear wild cry of the birds.

John Masefield
from "Tewkesbury Road"

As the summer moves steadily toward the locusts' awakening in August, one often wonders where more than half the year has so swiftly gone.

"Swifter than a weaver's shuttle," Job said of the days when his afflictions came upon him, "and spent without hope." Even if we do not have the troubles of Job to suffer, the flying shuttle in the weaver's hands as it crosses and re-crosses the warp on the loom and, by its passage, gradually creates the pattern of the finished material, seems a good image of our lives.

The threads of the warp, those threads that are strung upon the loom before the weaving proper is begun, represent the ground of our being, those qualities, both light and dark, that are already ours at the moment of conception. And the plying of the weaver's shuttle back and forth through the warp gradually forms the pattern of the material, representing the pattern of our days.

After a cold June, summer has arrived all of a sudden, in a humid rush.

When I take the dog out for his walk at the end of the evening, I see more fireflies than I can remember ever seeing here. They remind me of childhood summers in Pennsylvania, sitting, as dusk fell, with relatives on the big side porch of the house my great-grandfather built after the Civil War, a citronella candle burning to ward off mosquitoes, half-listening to the quiet talk and quieter pauses of the adults, the sound of the occasional car passing down the main street out front, the rhythmic squeak of the porch glider with its cushions that smelt of waterproofing, wondering at the bloom of firefly light amongst the overgrown shrubbery at the edge of the yard. We would check to see if it was high up ("Looks like the weather will be fair tomorrow") or lower down almost to the ground ("Looks like we might get some rain"). The conversation would go on to discuss the state of the crops and the pastures and a thousand details of life in the country.

This year, I wish the fireflies were flying lower. Although there has been rain nearby, and a good deal of it, we have gotten only tiny showers that barely register on the rain gauge. I must go out this evening and drag around some hoses attached to tiny sprinklers so as to give at least some of the plants a bit of relief from the drought. We've been carrying buckets of water daily to some trees we just planted, a clump of three, young white birch and a sand cherry. The birch clump is looking good, but a passing deer neatly nipped off the sand cherry's growing tips some nights ago.

So far, the deer have left Alice's garden alone but there are a great number of them in the neighbourhood and we no longer have a dog that feels strongly possessive about the whole property. We can't do much about the deer, short of getting into major fencing operations. But as far as rain is concerned, this might be a day to watch, thanks to the purported influence of a long-dead Bishop.

Today, the 15th of July, is Saint Swithin's day. If it rains today, as the saying goes, it will rain for the next forty. Of course, if it doesn't rain today, then it won't rain for the next forty. It's a not-so-old story. The first recorded evidence for it dates from the fourteenth century, five hundred years after the Bishop of Winchester's death.

Bishops in those days were close to their people and there is a lovely story of the Bishop who liked to sit for a while each day and watch a bridge being built. One day, as he was sitting there he saw one of the workmen maliciously bump an old woman carrying a basket of eggs. The eggs fell and broke. So the good Bishop caused the eggs to be made whole again.

That, of course, is something that "everyone knows" to be quite impossible, even for "all the king's horses and all the king's men." Is the story true? Well, who is to say? Why do we believe that strange things happen now, but deny that in times past saints could do what can't be done by us today?

Whether he mended the eggs or not, it is also said that Saint Swithin is the Saint to pray to in case of drought. That might be a good idea; unless, of course, the rain has visited us since I wrote this column.

Thomas Traherne spent his early life in the English county of Hereford, on the Welsh border, the son of a poor Welsh shoemaker. Thanks to the aid of wealthier relatives he went up to Oxford and, after graduating, returned to Hereford as an Anglican priest. His quiet life was disturbed only briefly when he was called to London to act as Chaplain to a Hereford nobleman. Eventually he became the vicar in a small village not far from London, and died there in 1674, at age thirty-seven, leaving behind the sum of five pounds, some clothing and a few books.

During his life, Thomas Traherne wrote a series of short reflections, collected in a notebook to send to a friend, Mrs. Susanna Hopkins, of Herefordshire. Never published, the notebook was discovered by chance in a bookseller's bin in the nineteenth century. It passed through several hands before coming into the possession of Bertram Dobell, a London publisher. In 1908, more than two hundred years after Traherne's death, Dobell published this work, calling it *Centuries of Meditations*, Traherne having written his reflections in groups of one hundred. *Centuries of Meditations* is one of the great spiritual classics of all time. One evening, over three hundred years after they were written, Traherne's words came to me in a special way.

As I was standing at the door to the paddock last night, waiting for the cows to come down from the orchard pasture, a Hayden quartet flowing quietly past me from the radio in the barn, and the black silhouettes of the trees at the edge of the field adding emphasis to the luminosity of a sky that, as yet, held only a half-moon and bright Jupiter, I thought of a passage of Traherne's that I had just copied out that afternoon:

When things are ours in their proper places, nothing is needful but prizing to enjoy them. God therefore hath made it infinitely easy to enjoy, by making everything ours, and us able so easily to prize them. Everything is ours that serves us in its place. The sun serves us as much as is possible, and more than we could imagine. The clouds and stars minister unto us, the World surrounds us with beauty, the Air refresheth us, the Sea revives the earth and us. The Earth itself is better than gold because it produceth fruits and flowers.

Standing there in the beauty of the evening, it came to me how right Traherne was, how much there is to prize in the world that bears us up and wraps us round with wonders, especially when we allow the things around us to be "in their proper places," and don't try to make them be something they are not, by forcing them to our will.

I had reason to rejoice and to give thanks. A recent encounter with an academic from Toronto had put me briefly in touch again with the university life and its incomprehension of all that is not part of its world.

He asked me what we grew on our "ginger ale farm." This dismissive question was a reference to our proximity to Sussex and its famous namesake beverage.

I have wondered ever since how I should have answered. But now, looking about me in the silvery evening, waiting for the cows to come in, I realized there were no words, no "Answer," definitive for all time, that the Professor would respond to. Rather, the answer came to me from everything around me; "Here we are. We are your answer. Be still. Attend. Listen, and watch."

A light breeze barely whispered in the woods across the paddock as I leaned against the door of the barn and heard the rich harmonies of the music from the radio. I absorbed without words, without even conscious effort, all the common, ordinary glory of an August evening here on this place, at this moment in time. And among all the impressions which came crowding in, I remembered the field below the road, the field which had been in imminent danger of growing up in brush, the field which thanks to a neighbour had been ploughed, limed, and seeded. What had been weedy pasture was now bare earth, the earth Traherne speaks of, "better than gold because it produceth fruits and flowers."

Peace be with you, Professor from Toronto. I'll follow Thomas Traherne.

...the way to become rich and blessed is ... to approach more near, or to see more clearly with the eye of our understanding, the beauties and glories of the whole world: and to have communion with the Deity in the riches of God and Nature.

I ran into a collection of haying pictures from our early years on the farm a while back. The haying had to be done and money was scarce. Our method of getting the hay in for the winter was certainly unorthodox, and like many of our imaginative approaches to farming, they were the sort of method guaranteed to astonish and entertain the neighbours.

We had bought an old Cockshutt ground-driven mower with the farm and were given an old rope hayloader. These became the basis of our haying operation every summer. I don't remember when it was that we had the mower converted to a rig that could be towed by our truck, but I do remember who did it—Wes Alcorn, a blacksmithing genius in Belleisle Creek. As far as I could determine, he could do anything and do it by eye.

He no doubt had had experience in the conversion of horse-drawn equipment to tractor-drawn before we appeared on the scene. He seemed to know by instinct just how to make the transition. As far as I remember, he never laughed at us or our methods, which were based on using what we had as others had done before us

After the mower was converted, we had to find a way to pull it. We didn't have a tractor so we hooked it up to the army truck we had bought and named Brutus. Brutus's virtue was that he could motor in low range and low gear at a speed our old equipment could stand. But Brutus was hardly light on his feet. His turning radius was just slightly under half a football field with the Cockshutt mower hooked on behind. The driver could only tell whether all was well by a slight vibration of the cab. Get the vibration just right and the driver knew the mower was running smoothly. But if the person riding the mower wished to communicate with the engineer in the cab it was necessary to have a relay interpreter in the box of the truck that could shout directions to the driver through the cab window.

We had a good crew in those days and we needed every one of them. One person rode the mower, usually Alice; one person kept Brutus on some kind of straight path, usually me; the kids shouted instructions, warnings, and encouragement from the box of the truck and from the field alongside our odd example of beating "swords into ploughshares."

How well I remember the way cars on the road would come to a virtual halt when they caught sight of Brutus, the mower, and the great cloud of witnesses who accompanied them about the field. No one ever drove off the road while gazing in astonishment, but I think that was more good luck than good management.

If the sight of Brutus pulling the little mower was wondrous, the sight of how we picked up the hay was equally wondrous. Here again Brutus was the star of the show, this time hauling an old rope hayloader, while one or two children tramped the hay as it fell into the box and others clustered around making sure the hay Brutus missed because of his turning radius got picked up and put on the loader.

The box on the army truck was not large, so many trips were required to pick up all the loose hay and transport it to the barn. The kids used to vie to see who could get the most hay stuffed into the box and, once the back window of Brutus's cab was covered there was no way for crew to communicate with driver, except by pounding on the roof of the cab. One thump meant stop and two thumps meant carry on—or maybe it was the other way around.

At the barn our methods were equally unorthodox. The truck backed in to the central threshing floor between the two haymows. We had acquired a hay pitcher and rope from an elderly neighbour, Harold Parlee, who had also taught us how to milk our first cow. The hay pitcher was a great labour-saving device once we got it strung up on the pulleys which still hung in the peak of the barn roof from when they had been put to the same purpose at least fifty years earlier. A borrowed tractor pulled the rope that lifted the clamshell-like device into the haymow. Here again, numbers of workers were needed to effect the transfer: one to dig the clamshell into the hay in the box of the truck, one up on a beam to pull the trip rope that let the load fall into the haymow (this was usually one of the younger children who enjoyed the thrill), another responsible worker to stand at the barn door to let the tractor driver know when he had pulled the load out of the truck and into the mow.

No, our methods were certainly not orthodox. But they worked.

We all know about Indian summer, that most poignant echo of things that used to be. Indian summer, with its warm sunny days and bright blue skies, seems to be a drawing back of nature's hand from the destruction she had been intending, and still intends, a kind of temporary stay of execution before the advent of winter.

The wind pursued the little bush,
And drove away the leaves
November left; then clambered up
And fretted in the eaves.

Emily Dickinson
from "At Home"

Fall is the great season in Canada. But, in fact, we don't have *a* fall, we have three different seasons that together make up fall. First, starting in September, comes the season of harvest and the red-green-gold fireworks of the maple trees. High winds sometimes mean an abrupt departure for the colours of the great going-out-of-business sale the maple trees put on every year. It's a beautiful show, but fleeting. Then, as October mounts the boards and the winds carry off the maple leaves, we have a season of bright blue skies and clear air, with the tamaracks in the woods turning a dull gold. Then, inevitable and sombre, November brings us a third fall season, with its grey skies and brown fields. This is when the spruce trees in their dark greens come to the fore and suddenly look quite festive. They were too subtle to have been noticed in summer or the riot of early fall. The landscape now glows with a richness that makes the flaring maples seem rather gaudy.

A professor of mine in college used to point out to us how much depends on what he called the "just noticeable differences." This is true in appreciating the landscape as well as poetry. William Carlos

William's tiny jewel of a poem, "The Red Wheelbarrow," is a perfect example of how just noticeable differences give much of poetry its tension and sense of inevitability.

so much depends
upon

a red wheel
barrow

glazed with rain
water

beside the white
chickens

In Williams' poem, it is the rhythm of the three-word lines against the one-word lines, and the openness of the first line that makes for the just noticeable differences. Williams could have written, "Everything depends" for his first line and had the same rhythm, but that statement is too sweeping, claims too much. The just noticeable difference between 'everything' and 'so much' is the difference between a memorable poem and a nice try.

Just noticeable differences surround us in the larger world as well, and they are just as hard to pin down there as they are in a poem.

How clearly certain moments stand out in memory, vivid flashes of time past that linger on the retina of the mind when all about them has faded into formlessness. Why it is I don't know, but for me November days have a special link with memory. It's then the very air seems to resonate with voices from the past as a great cathedral resonates with the sound of chanting long after the last Amen has ended. And the resonance is not just of private memories. The air seems to be alive, not only with the memories one's own mind has caught and held, but with presences that crowd in upon one in the pale light of the declining sun; as if all of the long history of this creation was calling, whispering in a voice just beyond the threshold of hearing, of things already old when Priam became king of Troy.

The Church, in its long pilgrimage through time, has listened to the many voices that echo through Creation, voices strong and weak, good and evil, and gives them all their due. Is it any wonder that All Hallows' Eve at the very end of October is the time when the forces of evil, seen as comic, seen as they really are and not as they would like to appear, have their fling? And is it any wonder that they are put to flight by the dawning of November and the Feast of All Saints, the feast particularly of that great cloud of witnesses whose sanctity was and is, daily and domestic, known but to a few and to God. November is a time to look carefully about and to ponder the voices carried faintly on the wind.

Right now, I think of autumn as leaves and sky, bringing with it a sense of the spirits of other times and other places that seem to crowd around me, plucking at my sleeve or jogging my memory.

Leaves first of all. Not leaves on the trees, for we have gone beyond the brilliant sunny reds and yellows of early autumn. Now the cows come into the barn of an evening with yellow-brown tamarack needles on their backs. A sharp frost several weeks ago signalled the end of the long sunny days of summer. In the space of six or seven hours our big maple tree dropped all but a few of its leaves and the ground around it shone with their reflected golden glow.

Listening to the whispering rustle, I walked through the leaves as they lay on the ground, and remembered, caught as if in amber, a particular sidewalk and a particular afternoon walk home from school one long-forgotten day, forty and more years ago. I can't say when, or give the name of the street, or recall which school I was walking from. All memory brought me was a moment, and the sidewalk;

but the sound of the leaves as I walked up under the maple tree to check the fence found me at once in two times, two places, and for a moment I did not know which was real, which was memory.

And again last week, returned from four days in Halifax, I was coming up from the barn in the late dusk of a rainy day, thinking how good it was to be here and not there, when the diamond water drops caught by the poplar leaves strewn over the driveway suddenly brought to mind a sunny late fall day in Akron, Ohio, a place I only visited once in my life and then only for a few short days.

What catches these moments? And where are they stored, to leap out at us all unawares like that? What just noticeable difference in our spirit or our surroundings puts times and places together, does its own poetry, and creates its own similes and metaphors? "See?" it says. "The leaves you are walking through now you have walked through before. The rain-washed pale blue of the sky tonight is like that other day long ago which you didn't even know you had noticed."

Autumn is no *déja vu* season. It isn't that we are struck with the feeling that we have done all this just this way already. The brilliant blue of September skies, the sense of more and more sky appearing as the trees lose their leaves, the innumerable, just noticeable, differences that tell us where we are in the year really are *déja vu*—we have seen them before—and yet the effect is always new. Always new, and yet, isn't there something in the earth and air around us that makes this the time for Halloween ghosts? Don't we all live in haunted houses?

There was often a great calm that came with late fall on the farm when at least some of the chores were completed. The garden was harvested, the hay was in the mow, the chickens could wander to their hearts' content, and much of the electric fence had been taken up and put away until spring. The cows—when they were out at all—were in the little paddock beside the barn, not because we needed to keep an eye on them but because there was nothing of any interest to them farther afield. I was then often reminded of a beautiful folk song:

All before me peaceful,
All behind me peaceful,
Under me peaceful,
Over me peaceful,
All around me peaceful.

Josh Bogin
based on a Navajo proverb

Those who have never had the experience can never know the intense and primitive satisfaction that comes on a stormy winter night to those who know they have plenty of food on hand and plenty of fuel.

George Woodbury
from *John Goffe's Mill*

Mornings in Advent are often white and frosty. Everything outdoors hangs with ice crystals flashing and burning with a million suns. It's a wonderful sight when we come to bottom dead centre of the sun's year, the winter solstice.

Two motions mark this season. On the one hand, the sun is apparently moving further and further away. On the other hand, this dark season—like the trees and shrubs and wild grasses on a frosty morning—seems to sparkle with a light beyond light.

"Real Christmas weather," I hear people saying. Why do we think of this as "real" Christmas weather? Why are icicles and frost on windowpanes and sleigh-bells the necessary symbols of an event that took place amid palm trees? Even in the southern US, where snow is a one-day wonder (if it falls at all), this time of year the stores are all decorated with tinsel and artificial snow and billboards proclaim a snow belt Bethlehem.

An old-fashioned Christmas speaks to us very forcibly. It speaks of change because we recognize the scenes, yet know they are not "now." It speaks of permanence because in recognizing the scenes we identify ourselves with them. Permanence in the midst of change, the stillness at the heart of endless agitation; whatever the grief and troubles that cluster about us, thick enough at the best of times, an old-fashioned Christmas speaks a silent language we hear even if we do not respond to the deeper message of the Church. Mystery has many voices and the inexpressible calls us at every level of our being, even, if need be, at the most superficial. Even tinsel, mindlessly thrown on an artificial tree, may be, for someone, a door.

It's nearly a decade since our family came here, intent, as city folk often are, on changing the world and doing it right now. The first winter's struggle with a wood pile of what seemed to be intractable stubbornness suggested that perhaps the new Jerusalem would not be born of sheer force of will. Now we walk to different rhythms and, if we are still hasty by local standards, I'm sure our city friends wonder why it takes us so long to do such simple things.

I recently found a list of "Things That Must Be Done Immediately," a list drawn up our first year here, and was impressed by the number of things that still remain to be done. It is good that it should be so; if all those tasks had been done, I would suggest that we had set our sights too low, had settled for cheap satisfaction and turned our backs on eternity. As it is, no doubt some of the things on the original list will still be there when our children take up where we leave off.

In the back of the barn—now piled high with an impressive collection of jute feed bags from the Co-op, bee equipment, a quarter horse electric motor, some old windows without glass, and goodness knows what else—

is a sleigh. We didn't buy it at an auction and lug it home to gussie it up and stick out on the lawn to look quaint. The sleigh is part of this place. We know stories about it and about the people whose place this was and for whom it is still named, just as the red farm wagon with the iron wheels and the horse drawn plough are part of this place, part of its history, part of the past but also part of the present. Our neighbours pulled into the yard the other day in a sleigh drawn by their big shire horse. Someday, perhaps, we will get out our sleigh, hitch up Gem and Sally, and return the call. Perhaps, when we return, we will find a babe, wrapped in swaddling clothes lying in the manger, with snow covering the ground, frost on the windows of the stable, and icicles hanging from the eaves.

When does a year start? And when does a year end? Do we have any more than a statistical indication?

Everybody since the introduction of the Gregorian calendar thinks January 1st is the beginning of the year. You don't find many New Year's parties being held in March anymore, the way they used to be. None of the kind shopkeepers who value my patronage and insist that I take their latest and most beautiful calendar are wont to pull a rolled-up piece of glossy stock out from under their counter in July and hand it to me with the words, "Have you got one of our calendars yet?" No doubt if they did there would be what the novelists like to call an awkward pause in the conversation.

Mind you, I could probably handle it. Just the other day I caught myself writing 1989 on a cheque, and months fall away from me like leaves on a windy October day. Years don't have the density of texture they used to have in my youth. Back then the distance between the first day of school and the last was, as Second Peter tells us, "one day is with the Lord as a thousand years."

It was also true that the distance between the first day of summer holidays and the beginning of school was just as infinitesimal in extent. Now, the whole 365 and 1/4 days of the year is like a running of the Queen's Plate, only I can't remember which horse I am betting on, and the whole lot of them are well out of the gate before I realize the finish line was just the starting gate in disguise.

Where did this odd notion come from that January 1st is the beginning of the year? Can you think of a dumber time to begin a new year? I suspect that January 1st got the nod because nobody could think of anything else to do with it and shopkeepers and factory hands thought it was too soon after Christmas to go back to work full time.

Anybody who looks at the names of the months at the "end" of the year will see they are really the seventh, eighth, ninth, and tenth months. It doesn't take a lot of calculating to figure out that the Romans, among others, began the year with March.

Further south than here, March makes a darn good time to start a year, marking as it does the coming of spring and the opening of a new agricultural season. Around here, the year begins on the Victoria Day weekend, it seems to me. Even though the lettuces and peas and other tough-minded seeds have been in the ground for quite a while before then, the neighbourhood of Victoria Day is sure to find most gardeners bent double over some furrow or other, committing seeds to the annual miracle of resurrection.

Years don't necessarily end back-to-back with beginnings either. As far as I was concerned when I was a child in school, something very like a year ended when school started again in the fall, and the next year didn't start until June, although there were some good bits scattered between September and June as well. Those days fell outside the year proper and so might be called intercalary, from the Latin word for day. They were inserted, like the 29th of February, between two others for some special purpose.

This past year ended the day before Christmas Eve on our farm because that was the day when, aided by a daughter home from one of the temples to higher learning, I finally finished the new chicken house. If you remember the weather that far back in time, you will recall that it had overtones of the Last Days, at least as the Last Days were played in the time of Noah. The heaviest rain that day came after dark, just when the biddies and their attendant roosters were being carried from the old coop to the new one. Judging from the comments, some of the roosters, especially, thought it wasn't just the year that was ending.

Now, we wait for a new year in the chicken coop. I figure it should come about the time the birds get over their shock and begin to reward us with the eggs our care and concern so clearly merit.

Oh—and by the way—Happy New Year to you too. That is, if you happen to be celebrating it around this time of year.

I happened to look down at the right sleeve of my sweater after returning from the morning milking the other day and was delighted to discover lots of short brown hairs sticking to it like so many infant porcupine quills. "Aha!" I said to myself. "The cows have started to shed their winter coats." And indeed, it was so. Outside it didn't look like spring, but the cows seem to know something. Spring is calling.

One of the fascinations in country life for someone from a metropolis is the inter-relatedness of created things. In the city, so many people live and work in such a small space that nature and her affairs are scarcely noticed until she does something quite out of the ordinary. In the country, though, people are not so thick on the ground and nature is a force to be watched carefully and cooperated with, if possible. Nature and humanity may not live entirely in harmony; there are rains when the hay is ready to come in and frosts before all the tomatoes are harvested. But we must reach for harmony, and the harmony of the heavens, earth, and humanity must be on nature's terms, however much the agribusiness boys would like to triumph over everything but their own greed.

My first experience of this inter-relatedness was the hectic pace of summer in New Brunswick. Everything outdoors had to be crammed into the brief time between the sun's swift rise to the height of heaven in late spring, and its equally rapid declension toward the south a few months later. How was it possible to do everything that had to be done in the brief time available? It all seemed like pushing fast-forward on the VCR.

I think the second experience was of the reality of the wintertime condition called "cabin fever." *A Dictionary of Canadian English* that I once consulted listed "cabin fever" as a true Canadianism. It quoted an account of a logging camp in which the cook, "suffering from cabin fever," arose one night, fried every egg in the camp to a state of leather and nailed each and every fried ugly to the cookhouse wall. Having experienced New Brunswick winters with a house full of kids, dogs and cats, my heart goes out to that cook. Even Torontonians occasionally suffer cabin fever.

Although Toronto is sometimes called "Muddy York," it was only after we came to New Brunswick that we learned the term and the meaning of the multiple appearances of the aptly named "mud season."

Only gradually do patterns take shape behind all these experiences. Weather patterns come first, I think. cloud shapes and wind directions gain significance and names. Still fall evenings, when the sky is clear and the barometer bounds upward, make the gardener reach for the old sheets to protect the precious produce from frost. The moon's phases, especially the date of the full moons in June and September, when frost is quite possible, are not just abstractions in an Almanac.

Watching the moon as it wanders, now high in the sky, now low, now early, now later in appearance, one discovers that the stars themselves move with dignity across the sky, the realm of what our elders called the "fixed stars." There I saw for myself the energetic planets, those wanderers through the zodiac. I saw for myself Mars stop in his course, then go back upon his path, only to stop again and then continue his forward progress. Later still, standing outside the barn in the evening, I began to recognize the constellations that blazed above me, watched them and used their progress from week to week to measure both the duration of one season and the coming of the next.

What a sense of the transience of all earthly things accompanies the first sighting of the constellation Orion, winter's king, above the eastern horizon as fall enters its middle age. Months later, and with expectation, one follows the curve of the Big Dipper's handle and suddenly recognizes bright Arcturus, harbinger of summer, rising in the east even though the ground is still locked in winter's rigour.

Some of these patterns can be glimpsed from within cities, but only glimpsed. For the most part, they remain bookish fancies that can be picked up for a moment and then dropped again when the moment passes. The reality of these seasonal patterns—the reality of the force of a winter storm borne on the back of a furious east wind or the reality of the effect of a full moon in September on the ripening tomatoes—remains a literary reality at best. Our cows, now shedding their winter coats, are not interested in metaphors. They know the time and the seasons.

Chapter 6: Cattle After Their Kind

All the really good ideas I ever had came to me while I was milking a cow.

Grant Wood

Life on a farm is often mistakenly seen as slow, calm, and quiet; the view from many roads around Kings County amplifies this stereotype. Cattle graze in broad pastures, issuing the occasional, quiet "moo." Their most energetic movements no more than a slow walk to another patch of green, or the flick of a tail to swat away the flies.

Passers-by see nothing but serene views of a herd with large barns and silos in the distance as mere decoration instead of the symbols of hard work and daily labour that they really are. I can't blame them. Until moving to the farm, even I was guilty of these kinds of ideas from time to time.

Oh, did the cows change my mind! Reality with these characters was anything but calm.

Because of the way the house and barn are laid out on our farm, our cows spend part of their time on the opposite side of the house from the barn, over in the field with the old apple orchard. Years ago, we used to turn the animals into the pasture behind the house, which was called the "night pasture" by the original owners because it kept the cattle close to the barn for morning milking.

For several summers now, we have put the night pasture off limits to the cows, hoping that a bit of a rest might effect a change for the better in the quantity and quality of grass there. All the cows see of it, is a rather narrow laneway that gets them from the paddock beside the barn, past the granary, back behind the old chicken house and drive shed, up past the big maple tree, and into the orchard pasture. As I suspected, they spend very little time in the laneway, being much more interested in the long grass in the orchard.

The resulting configuration of pasture and paddock looks something like one of those mazes the men in the white suits are always dropping mice into to see whether they can figure out where the cheese is. In order for the cows to get back to the paddock at milking time they must initially move away from the barn in the direction of the night pasture and negotiate several twists and turns in the laneway before they can see the barn ahead of them.

It does no good to stand outside the barn and call them, even though we, and they, all know it's milking time. If they hear us calling, they simply come to the point in the orchard closest to the barn and stand peering over the fence looking glum

By virtue of this state of affairs we arrive at one of the pleasant tasks of the day called "bringing in the cows." It's a meditative activity, once the cows are rounded up and convinced you mean for them to go to the barn, giving one the opportunity to observe earth and sky, to listen to the songs of the birds, and to ponder whatever it is that seems worth pondering at the time.

Cows are not much given to haste, so the trip is at a contemplative pace. If the herdsman is inclined to pause to investigate an unfamiliar plant or flower or to listen for the song of the wood thrush or just to admire the clouds in the blue sky, the cows are quite content to stop and think their slow ruminative thoughts as well, taking up their progress again when urged to do so.

The observer, at this season, is well advised to cast their eye upon the ground along the laneway. The wild strawberries—startling flecks of crimson in the greens and browns of the short grass—are ripening. One of the children, along on a recent morning excursion to bring in the cows, observed that one tiny wild berry has all the flavour of the cultivated berry twenty times its size.

The part of the night pasture that remains uncolonized by alders seems also the poorest in terms of the plants that it will grow on this site. Even goldenrod there is sparse and small. Instead, on the dry, sunny bank sloping to the southwest beside the drive shed, we have drifts of mouse-ear hawkweed with its pretty dandelion-like lemon coloured blooms raised above the surrounding thin grass on long, fuzzy stems. A little further down the slope, an abundance of the little white star blossoms of the wild strawberries give promise of delights to come.

I know the hawkweed is what its name implies, a weed. I know it is bent on taking over whatever land it can by forming mats of creeping runners and spreading its flat rosette of leaves tight against the ground so as to discourage other plants more acceptable to the cows and the farmer. But it is an ancient plant, companion of humans over thousands of years. The Greek Dioscorides, living in Asia Minor, knew it and included it in his *Materia Medica* sometime in the first Christian century. Pliny the Elder, who perished in the eruption of Mount Vesuvius in 79 AD, mentions in his *Historia Naturalis* that hawks feed upon the plant to sharpen their eyesight. The Middle Ages knew it as Auricula muris, "Mouse Ear." Great herbalists of nearer times, John Gerard (*The Herball or the General Historie of Plantes*, 1597) and Nicolas Culpeper (*The English Physician Enlarged*, 1653) both valued the hawkweed.

The strawberry, a humble member of the rose family, uses the same method of propagation as the mouse-ear hawkweed, and are found nearly everywhere in the Northern Hemisphere. It's a reminder to the farmer that the soil where they grow is acidic and needs lime.

This little plant too has the dignity of long association with humanity and seems to have been especially dear to the English. A thousand years ago the "streawberige" appeared in an English herbal now preserved in a manuscript in the British Museum. It appears as "straberie" in a household account of the Duchess of Leicester in the thirteenth century. "Strabery ripe!" was the cry in the streets of London in the fifteenth century, as the poet Lydgate reminds us. Ben Jonson mentions them in a play written at the beginning of the seventeenth century. Even Mother Goose tells of a suitor who promises Curly-locks that she shall "...sit on a cushion / And sew a fine seam, / And feed upon strawberries, / Sugar and cream."

So, I take my time to admire the hawkweeds and the strawberries in their own part of the pasture. With only a few cows we are not under the heavy economic pressures of commercial farming and feel free to invoke legend and beauty as goods, above the good of strict utility.

Bringing in the cows is a time in and out of time. The time of day, the weather, the whole knot of life from the herbs and tiny creatures underfoot, to the swallows dipping and swooping in the air overhead, to the moving pattern of cloud and blue sky, it is all one moment and only one moment, unique, never having happened before and never to be just this way again. As the cows and I pause to greet the green wanderers through time and space at our feet—friends and associates of the human journey down thousands of years—chores and the day's demands are in abeyance, suspended in a momentarily distant future.

"How do we stop this thing?" I asked over my shoulder.

Alice had come into the barn to show our guests around while I was seated on the milking stool filling a pail with the finest of Jersey milk.

"Good heavens," she said. "All that?"

"All that," in this case, meant nearly a full pail of milk from a cow who was supposed to have been dried off a week before. Conflicting emotions always assail me when the time comes to dry the cow off, especially when there is only one cow to milk. Part of me thinks ahead to six or eight weeks of being able to come and go without reference to milking time. Part of me thinks back to our first cow and my discovery of the routine as a pleasant thing. That part of me rather regrets the temporary loss, which always reminds me that there will come a time when we will no longer keep a cow. For the moment though, concerns of that sort receded before a concern that this cow was not going to stop producing milk—ever.

Maggie is the first cow we have milked that was born on this farm and we have always gotten along quite well. Other years, there has been no argument about The End. By the time she should be dried off so as to put her energies into the coming calf, she and I have been in agreement that a halt should be called.

Usually, for a week or so before the end, I drop back to milking once a day. The first couple of times I get the equivalent of the evening and the morning milking all in the one pail. But then the wheels begin to turn, and Maggie figures out that I am trying to tell her something. The next day there is less milk and the next day still less, and so on. By the end of the week the halt has all but been called.

The next few days she stays outside, if the weather is fair. We keep an eye on her to make sure something nasty like mastitis doesn't appear, but otherwise, the milking routine is at an end. Then she is officially a dry cow and entitled to all the rights and privileges thereunto pertaining.

This year, however, not only did Maggie perform really well, she was still performing really well when the time came to call a halt. We dropped back to one milking a day and after seven days she was still producing the equivalent of both milkings at one milking.

"Why have we been bothering to milk twice a day all these years?" Alice asked, as I trudged up from the barn with yet another pail full of golden milk. Why indeed? But what was going on? Why wasn't my normally swift cow getting the picture?

Each morning I would let her back into the pasture, to spend her time bossing her offspring around, telling them exactly what they could and could not do, eat, or investigate, and when and where they could or could not do it. Until the next morning all she could expect from us was water. I even cut back a bit on the water supply and moved them all onto the poorer pasture. But the milk kept flowing.

There had to be a reason. I stopped milking entirely for several days and watched for signs of an explosion. The udder in question looked full but not too full. Maggie seemed quite calm. After four days I decided to milk once more, just to empty out what was still there.

It was at that point that Alice came into the barn and clapped her hand to her brow in amazement. What I got was nice fresh milk in just the amount I had last gotten four days before.

There is a group of birds, including the Whip-Poor-Will and the Nightjar or Nighthawk, known as goatsuckers because they were thought to milk goats with their large mouths. Could it be that our back pasture had suddenly become infested with goatsuckers turned cowsuckers?

And then at last, the penny dropped. Into my mind flashed a memory of my kindly wife actually hurling a missile at our steer the year before when she caught him, at age one and a bit, tanking up on some illicit milk. When I finished milking that night, I put Maggie out one door, and the steer and the heifer out the other to separate pastures. That was two days ago; and Maggie's doing fine, all by herself. What's more, milk production has ceased. John Steer is looking woeful, as well he might.

There are some animals I don't warm up to. My wild and wonderful aunt, who used to send me subscriptions to terribly avant-garde literary periodicals, developed an affinity for Chows when I was about knee-high to a grasshopper. I don't see many Chows these days, but then, come to think about it, I didn't see many back then either.

That didn't bother me, I may say, because Aunt Kitty's Chows were more than enough.

In case you were wondering, a capital C Chow is a fair-sized dog that used to belong only to emperors in China. Some people called them Chow Chows, which seems silly. My dictionary tells me they are "a Chinese breed of medium-sized dogs having a thick, black, blue, red, or cream coat and a black tongue." They are definitely not to be confused with chow-chow, which is a New Brunswick green tomato relish.

Aunt Kitty had several Chows before her interest eventually waned. They were kept, as I recall, sequentially, which meant that from beginning to end of the Chow phase a lot of time had passed. Each of the dogs in the sequence was named Ching.

They didn't seem to mind being indistinguishable from some eponymous ancestor. (Go ahead, look up eponymous; I'll just wait here until you come back… There. Use the word three times today and it is yours for life. No charge.) As I was saying, before you rushed off to the dictionary, Aunt Kitty's Chows were all named Ching, which was the only good thing about them as far as I was concerned. And I often complained to the adults around me, that one had growled at me, or snarled, or generally told me to shove off and mind my own business.

What Webster's doesn't say about Chows is that none of them could be confused with a green tomato relish, nor would the term marshmallow be appropriate. Maybe the emperors had problems with crowd control or people running up all the time and asking for their autograph. If they did have these problems originally, they certainly didn't after they started keeping Chows.

A Chow does not look upon the human race with undisguised admiration. In fact, they don't look on anything with undisguised admiration. Taciturn is a word that can be used to describe the Chow. The only thing a Chow has clearly in mind is that anybody other than it and its owner is unnecessary. There are no shades of grey in a viewpoint like that. It wasn't that they were mean; they just didn't like anybody other than Aunt Kitty, and beyond that could not distinguish friend from foe.

I never got the better of any of the Chings, but I once did get the better of a steer who wasn't one of my favourite people either. This steer—we'll call him the evil Bernstein because that was his name—lived in a pasture belonging to friends of ours. One summer, our friends wanted to go away for several days and we volunteered to feed their animals, including the evil Bernstein.

Bernstein didn't really need any food, having plenty of grass in his pasture, but it was necessary to cross his pasture to feed the pigs who were penned up at the lower end to clean out some bushes. The evil Bernstein seemed to resent this daily trek through his pasture with food that was not being brought to him. He took to lying in wait at the corner of an alder thicket just where the path came out into the pasture. If you were going along thinking what a nice evening it was or perhaps thinking about something nice that you were going to do after you slopped the hogs, suddenly there would be the evil Bernstein doing this Toreador Act and you had to look pretty lively for a moment. It wasn't that he was mean exactly; he just had a rather warped sense of humour.

Anyway, one night I decided I had had enough. I started down the path as usual, but part way along I turned off into the alders and did a "Last of the Mohicans" routine kitty-corner down through the bush. It was one of the few times I have ever succeeded at this sort of thing. The evil B. was in his spot, as quiet as could be and smiling an evil smile. All his limited attention was focussed on the end of the path as I leapt out of the alders behind him and whapped him on the rump with a "yee-ha."

Consternation is not a typical bovine emotion, but consternation was Bernstein's response. I do believe he did zero to sixty in about six seconds, and some of his black spots went permanently white. He never played "pop goes the weasel" at the bottom of the path again.

I don't know how it is in large herds, but your family cow has a way of making her opinions clearly known without ambiguity.

We have had a number of cows of greater or lesser personality over the years. Brownie, our first cow, was already well advanced in years when she came to live with us. She taught us a lot about Jerseys in particular and cows in general. She had to. When she arrived, we had never milked a cow. Indeed, we had never had more than a passing acquaintance with a cow.

Our good neighbour, Harold Parlee, introduced us to the mysteries of milking as seen from the farmer's perspective. Brownie, a philosophical Jersey, endured the lengthy process without complaint although it was some time before she knew us well enough to be gracious about letting down the milk.

Brownie put up with a lot in those early days. It seemed that milking took hours; there were so many things to think about: how to sit, how to hold the bucket, how to reach under the udder to get the teats on the far side, how to squeeze. Every squirt of milk in the bucket was a hard-won victory. And this all had to be done twice a day! How did anyone who had to milk several cows ever get anything done? Through it all, Brownie would munch away at her hay and occasionally swing her head around and stare at the perspiring milker as if to say, "Why are you making such a fuss about such a simple process? Why don't you just get on with it?"

Brownie had a sense of humour. She was not given to slapstick comedy but every now and then, when the mood was on her, she would do the odd little thing. One of her favourite gags involved her grain pan.

We had decided that we had enough to do to learn to milk without having to pursue a cow who was herself

"...with her grain pan nicely upside down on her head like an Easter bonnet."

pursuing every last bit of grain we had put down in the trough in front of her. Finally, we bought a dishpan and used that for her grain ration, which did help to keep her more-or-less in one place. Gradually we began to get the hang of milking and the process seemed to grow more manageable and we learned how to adjust for the cow's movements.

Then, one morning, I noticed how nicely Brownie was standing, how quietly. I glanced up to discover her placidly chewing her cud, with her grain pan nicely upside down on her head like an Easter bonnet. She repeated this stunt several times over the years. How she did it, we never knew. By the time we noticed, it was already done. However it was done, it seemed to be her way of letting the world know that she could see the humour in things too.

It was also Brownie who, after she had been here for a couple of years and we had all gotten to know each other, suddenly, one day, gave us some anxious hours we won't soon forget. The incident happened after we decided that Brownie was getting too old and it was time to get another cow. We finally found one we could afford, another Jersey from near Fredericton. We borrowed a neighbour's truck to bring her home. Nothing, of course, had been said to Brownie who was out in the pasture when we left. As far as we knew the whole affair was not news, but when we got back with the new cow our old cow had vanished.

There are cows who simply do not respond well to confinement, but this had never been a problem with Brownie. For the whole of her first summer with us she had been on a tether and even that had not been a problem. But now, incredibly, she was nowhere to be found. It wasn't that she had found herself on the wrong side of the fence—she was just gone. Period. We called and called. A neighbour came over and helped us search. No Brownie.

We were all standing out between the barn and the granary, looking at the woods and feeling anguished. Night was coming. There didn't seem to be anything we could do. And then, for some reason I turned around. Not five feet from me stood Brownie. None of us had heard a thing. We never knew where she had come from.

Somehow, though, we felt she had expressed her opinion about bringing another cow into her barn.

One of the things I really like about our Jersey cows is their deviousness. Maybe our cows aren't the only devious ones. Cows may all be devious for all I know; it's just that I don't happen to have any really close friends in herds other than ours. Besides, I think Jerseys come with a bump of deviousness well developed, probably because they are smarter than a lot of other cows and have read more.

Deviousness is something all of us descendants of that pair of orchard thieves have absorbed in large measure, and so we just naturally recognize the same endearing trait in the so-called "lower orders." Frankly, I don't know what's particularly "lower" about a bunch of bovines whose ancestors for how many thousands of years have gone on peacefully eating grass and who now, here in the north country, have the self-styled "lord of creation" out on the back forty working like crazy to put in enough hay so they can go placidly on eating and complaining about the lack of room service for the nine months of the year when there is no grass outside.

Our deviousness must be the result of some chromosome somewhere down in the works that got a permanent crank when God applied the old boot to the seat of the fig leaves of the departing culprits and hung up the "No Snakes Allowed – Closed for the Season" sign over the main gate of "Jehovah's Botanical Park and Peaceable Kingdom." I was going to say that we absorbed deviousness with our mothers' milk, but as far as I have been able to tell those who were bottle-fed become just as devious as those who were breast-fed.

Human beings are so devious they seem to enjoy piling one outrageous activity on top of another. The thinking seems to be, that if what's going on looks pretty far out, chances are no one will really notice what's going on farther back and deeper in.

But with cows, their notion of deviousness is so wonderfully and refreshingly transparent. All you've got to do is watch closely and you can see the wheels turning. I wouldn't go so far as to say that an obscure smile plays around the corners of their lips, but there is definitely something about a cow who thinks she is getting away with something that says right out there in big letters, "I am getting away with something and you don't know what it is."

That's usually where she's wrong of course. Anything as devious as a human being can spot deviousness in the dark. Right now, our cows have got what they think is a real wheeze going and I can tell that it just tickles them pink to think they are getting away with it. In fact, it's giving them so much pleasure I wouldn't for the life of me let it show I was on to them.

The scam started a while back when we were running through our supply of good hay just a bit faster than spring was making its way north. We have a supply of hay that, to be devious about it, is aged to the point of being geriatric. A couple of times I put some of the geriatric hay down at milking time and was met with stares of blank disbelief. "You surely don't expect us to eat that?' they said, speaking as if with one voice.

Well, I did, but they wouldn't. And that was that. It had to be the good hay or nothing. That continued until the paddock reappeared from under the snow and dried out to the point that the cows could go out without needing snorkels to get through the mud. Then, I threw half a bale of the geriatric hay over the fence into the paddock thinking they might enjoy lying down on it.

Nothing could have been further from their minds. This hay was something they had found for themselves and the thing to do was to eat it all as fast as possible before we found out what they were up to and took it away from them.

So for the last week we've been tossing hay into the paddock and letting them think they've found something we don't know about. Meanwhile, the good hay is lasting nicely since we don't have to feed quite as much of it in the barn.

Deviousness is wonderful stuff, sometimes.

We are into our third mud season of the year on this hillside and the sap is running nicely. What's more, the water has been running in the barn since late February.

Our maple sugaring operation consists of nine spiles. Our sugar bush, if I may dignify it with that term, consists of one "gen-u-ine" sugar maple and a passel of swamp maples along an old fence line.

Yes, yes, we know. Nobody in his right mind taps swamp maples. That's all very well as far as it goes, but the convenience of a swamp maple on the fence line just beyond the orchard is worth ten sugar maples in the back forty, assuming there are ten sugar maples back there, which there aren't. So we get enough sap from our collection of trees to make all the maple syrup we can use before it's time to tap out next year.

Maybe the colour isn't light enough to win us a prize at the county fair and maybe someone who really knows maple syrup would smile bleakly if offered a taste and turn away in sorrow. Our syrup tastes just fine on pancakes. If we win no prizes for aesthetics, we hardly notice when pancakes are rushed to the table and thoughts of dollar bills fleeing away never cross our minds as we ladle just a dollop more syrup on the stack.

It's not just the sap that's running around here. Emotions are also running high among the barn cats, rather to the mystification of our splendid but purely decorative Thomas-Not-a-Tom who continues to focus closely on food and making sure he gets more than his fair share.

Thomas has acquired a new title, thanks to an off-the-wall novel Alice was reading a while back. Part of the action was set in a vegetarian restaurant with Buddhist overtones in San Francisco in the sixties. Need I say more? You can probably make up the plot yourself. Anyway, this restaurant had a cat named "The Ever Present Fullness." Well, names like that don't turn up every day of the week and when one does present itself it would be the worst sort of consumerism not to recycle it. Thomas positively basks in the implications.

The two calves who have been getting their milk from the source had gotten so big I finally decided it was time to wean them. In other years, when there was only one calf to deal with at a time, the logistics of weaning were simpler. This pair have had the freedom of the big box stall and it was obvious that calf B was not going to stand idly by while calf A was being introduced to a new food source.

Eventually I tied them in opposite corners of the stall and advanced with buckets. Jerusha, the heifer, was all for leaving to go see mommy, and although I had her backed into the corner we managed to spread milk about with reckless abandon. It reminded me of the comedy sketch in which the fellow doesn't know where the gas cap is on his new car and tells the station attendant "just pour the gas over the top; maybe it will run in someplace."

The other calf, Frank, was much easier to deal with. Like Thomas, Frank is not one to question the source of supply as long as the supply lasts. I dipped a couple of fingers in the milk, applied them to Frank's mouth, lowered his nose into the bucket, and we were off and running. Now and then he emerged from the deeps, snorting and blowing milk far and wide, but generally we were in business. I left the pen with a good deal of the milk I had brought in but distributed differently. I quietly congratulated Frank for demonstrating the natural superiority of the male.

In the evening, however, it turned out that Jerusha's objection was not to milk in a pail but to me putting my fingers in her mouth. I left her with the bucket and tried the same experiment with Frank. He stuck his nose in the pail and then came up wild eyed, looking for fingers.

A week later, Frank is still devoted to my fingers and me. Jerusha finishes her bucket by herself and without spilling a drop.

"It just shows the natural superiority of the female," Alice explained when I told her.

Talking about weaning calves reminds me again that the world divides and re-divides itself on any issue that may come down the pike, however un-dividable it might seem at first glance.

I originally discovered this penchant for hauling up on two sides of any issue when I was young and, incautiously as it turned out, assumed that everyone loved the operettas of Gilbert and Sullivan as much as I do.

G and S had swum into my ken in maybe eighth grade. Until recently I have opined that there was nothing redeeming in my entire experience of Junior High School that, for me, was more like the Chateau d'If. But the other day I was talking to someone about G and S and it suddenly came to me that I had had a wonderful music teacher back then who had introduced her class to *H.M.S. Pinafore* one year and to the *Mikado* the next. Her name has gone from me, apparently beyond recall, but I salute her as the one redeeming feature of the embodiment of Wordsworth's "shades of the prison house."

It came as a great surprise to me to discover, some years later, that the whole world did not share my enthusiasm, and, I must say, I still find it hard to believe. Ever since that discovery was forced on me, I have been keeping mental notes of inexplicable divisions we humans insist on, like the dogmatic disputes over weaning calves.

We have not had all that many calves to deal with since our farm is what the British would call a "smallholding," but neither Alice nor I had been brought up on farms where the weaning of calves was simply something on which God (or father) had pronounced in the beginning and it was thus done ever after. So, when we first were confronted with a calf that needed to break the mummy habit, we turned to a slim volume called *The Cow Economy*. Where we first came across this book I don't remember, but it is the best help a small operation like ours could ever wish for. It provides just the amount of information needed without sinking you in tables, charts, and cross sections of the stomach.

Not only did *The Cow Economy* discuss the pros and cons of keeping the calf with the cow for more than a few days (better not, unless you are so blessed with land that you can afford to keep cow and calf in separate fields more-or-less for ever), but it also discussed the pros and cons of different weaning strategies such as buckets with nipples vs. plain buckets.

Without realizing we were standing at a fork in the road of life, we followed our authors' lead and set out for the barn with an ordinary bucket, prepared for whatever might come. As I recall, what came was some awkwardness about getting a grip on the nose of the calf so that one's fingers were in the mouth. During this struggle, another member of the family guarded the bucket against spillage. I can't remember how many of us it took to wean that first calf, but we would probably have filled the local arena.

I do vividly remember the moment, not long after, when the calf wacked the bucket the way he was accustomed to wacking mother when the milk supply seemed to be getting scarce. What the physics of the act might be I don't know, but I do know that the milk remaining in the pail instantly gathered itself together and shot upward with great force, catching me just under the chin. From thence it divided, a portion proceeding upwards to make a good try at drowning me, whilst the majority took a sharp right and disappeared down the neck of my coveralls, headed, no doubt, for my boots, but contenting itself with producing a miasmal swamp that reached from neck to knees.

That pretty effectively ended Lesson One. It would be hard to say whether the calf or we learned more. Subsequently, we learned to back the calf of the hour into a corner so that his tendency to leave unexpectedly was thwarted, and we learned to keep a firmer hold on the bucket. The geyser effect has not been vanquished but we are better at ducking than we were.

That calf, and his successors, have all grown up to be happy, healthy, and productive members of society, as far as we can tell. However, we learned just last week that Dire Results ensue from this method of weaning. Apparently, the Only Way to wean is with a nipple pail which enables the calf to keep its head up and thus the milk goes into the right stomach, etc., etc. "You pays your money and takes your chances," in this as in other things, it seems.

One Sunday evening in June several years after we had moved here, I was returning from an evening service at a nearby Church and stopped off to have tea with a member of the parish and her family. The sky above me was blue with a pale citron sunset behind me to the west. Ahead, however, a dark line above the low hills spoke of a summer storm coming our way.

As I was driving back to the farm, I thought about how we were becoming serious hobby farmers, if not more than that. Without entirely intending to do so we had now acquired three Holsteins, a couple of Jerseys, and a Whiteface heifer. We were on our way.

The storm met me as I was coming over the mountain that rises behind the farm. The rain began sheeting down and my vision clouded as though I had suddenly grown cataracts. Through all the drumming of the rain, however, sharp flashes of light and instantaneous thunder surrounded me as the car nosed down the drenched highway. This was more than a passing summer storm. This was the sort of storm that would make you throw your hands over your head and run for cover if were you to be caught outside when it broke, the sort of storm about which a person might say that it "meant business."

As I turned onto our road, I wondered momentarily how the cows were making out. All the cows but one of the Jerseys, who had freshened the day before, had been put into the field that lies below the road and bisects our property. Because the way the farm lies, long and narrow with the road cutting across it about a third of the way down its length, there is not enough pasture to keep six cows above the road where the house and barn are set. This was the first year we had pastured cows below the road. Since that field was big, the cows had plenty of forage. Still, I did not envy them, being out in this deluge.

At home, our eldest daughter was sitting out on the front porch watching the progress of the storm. "Wow!" she said. "I think a bolt of lightning hit down below the road." By that time, the fiercest part of the storm was over, the thunder was growing more and more distant, and we thought no more about it. The rain gradually tapered away to a shower. It was going to be a lovely evening after all.

The next day began like the first day of Creation, cool with just the hint of a breeze. The sky was the pale blue of a robin's egg from which the baby robin had just hatched, and a light mist rose from the fields below us. In the valley beyond, white fog was lifting as if the Creation had not quite been completed when the sun first rose, and the wraps had yet to be taken off.

We looked down the field across the road for sight of our herd but saw no one. This was not particularly surprising since the field dipped halfway down to the stream that was its southern boundary. Below the dip our whole herd of cattle could pasture without being seen from the house.

It was only when our daughter came weeping up from the field where she had gone just to make sure that the electric fence was still working and the cows still behind it that we knew something was terribly wrong. I went to see for myself and found death in the heart of the smiling day. Four of the five cows that were in the pasture the night before would never require pasture again. All three Holsteins—Audrey, Bede, and Sweet Pea—lay underneath a yellow birch looking as if they would get up at any moment. Sweet Pea was due to calf in a month. The little Whiteface, Felicity, had been thrown twenty feet or so and lay with her neck twisted unnaturally to the side. Only our young Jersey, very distraught, was still on her feet. Her name, interestingly enough, was Faith.

That was the end of pasturing cows below the road. It was the end, too, of our growing herd. Since then, we have kept only one cow and a couple of young animals, the offspring of the current cow, until it was time either to sell them or put them in the freezer.

A week or so after the lightning storm, I went back to look at the spot. The birch tree obviously had not acted as a lightning rod. It had a few curls of scorched bark but nothing more. Behind the tree, however, was one of those rock piles, which are such a feature of cleared land in this country. There, I found a slight depression maybe ten feet across where rocks had been thrown aside from the force of the bolt. All I could imagine was that the pile contained an old ploughshare or some other bit of ancient cast-off metal that had attracted the lightning.

The birch tree continues to flourish. The depression in the rock pile is still there and will always be a reminder that within nature's realm are forces we can scarcely comprehend, let alone control, and that are always part of real life on a farm.

When we came here to take up what has sometimes been oddly called "the simple life" we had a fairly dewy-eyed approach to what the agri-business magazines call "the stock." Anybody who was raised on ads that featured Elsie the Borden cow will know what I mean. Elsie was a lady. Elsie was contented. Elsie moved in the best circles. A dark or greedy thought would never have crossed her mind. She was clean, dignified, and a model of selfless devotion to us milk drinkers.

The moral and ethical status of other barnyard habitués presented in media and children's literature was less clear. Chickens, as presented to us city kids in such award-winning dramas as the story of Chicken Little, left a great deal to be desired as stimulating company. Hickety-Pickety ("my black hen / who lays eggs for gentlemen"), however, seemed to have a bit more class, although she tended to be a trifle calculating. One felt that these days she might have had a sign out suggesting that she gave fair exchange on the U.S. dollar.

Pigs got mixed reviews. For those of a statistical bent, the story of the three little pigs implied that two out of three pigs were stupid. But, let's be frank here. While the third little pig could not be called stupid, I never understood why he couldn't have looked after his family a little bit better.

Ducks, of course, were treated pretty well by the media. Ping was independent of mind but things worked out pretty well for him. Then there is the song about the "one little duck, / with the feather on his back" who led the others with his "quack, quack, quack." I thought that was a pretty dumb song, to tell you the truth. I had never heard of a bald duck and any other duck was bound to have a good deal more than one feather on top. Anyway, it was a song that only came into the conversation if you were in the company of a gaggle of Girl Guides or with graduates of Camp Blaisdell, a summer camp for girls that purveyed some of the most revolting songs ever penned. My wife, Alice, went there, that's how I know.

I liked the story of the Three Billy Goats Gruff, but mainly because I liked to roar out "WHO'S THAT TRAMPING ON MY BRIDGE?" in a trollish voice, which was popular with the children. It was good to see the troll get his comeuppance when the biggest billy goat made the scene, but somehow the story never seemed to tell me much about the mind of the goat. This is fortunate, as I have since found out; I don't think children should be told anything about the mind of a goat.

Last week, however, I was forced to rethink the whole question of barnyard ethics. Maybe all the moral laxity that has been such a feature of daily news has infected even the "stable" world that Elsie the cow used to dwell in.

One morning that seemed like every other morning, all the cows refused to have anything to do with the loose hay put down for them. They looked at me when I sat down to milk, but they wouldn't eat. The whole lot of them looked shifty-eyed to me. Was there a problem with the hay? We'd had some baled hay delivered the day before as a safeguard against running out of our own loose hay before the winter was over. As a couple of bales had broken during delivery, I had fed some of that the evening before, which they had eaten.

Muttering, I offered the cows some more of the bought hay and, slurp, it was gone. Still muttering, I cleaned the loose hay out of the manger and went off to the house. There was a good deal of loose hay still in the mow, and now enough baled hay to last.

Milking time came, and I put down loose hay. A stony silence ensued. The shifty-eyed look had become hardened, steely. No contented cows, no meditative munching. Pretending a calm I was far from feeling, I addressed them thus: "Look, girls," I said. "That's it, eat it or starve." Nothing happened. It was a gloomy milking time. I left the barn wondering what we were going to do with all that spurned hay, including the stuff still in the mangers.

Apparently, there was a quick conference after I left the barn. That shifty-eyed look had been the look of co-conspirators. When I came down the next morning the mangers were bare. Nothing more has been said about not eating what is set before you.

I really don't think Elsie would have behaved like that.

It was around nine-thirty in the evening, or a little later, when I got to the barn. Our cow and the young steer, who just that morning had been moved into a new pasture, were not waiting at the door. Since our schedule does not tie us to any outside constraints, we can enjoy a more relaxed milking routine than observed on most other farms. If one or other party to the agreement is a bit early or late, nobody's nose will be out of joint.

This cow has come back to stay with us for the summer. At a moment of need last fall, when we thought we would have to sell her, friends with a small farm much like ours came to say they would be happy to keep her through the winter if we could take her back in the summer. So Mirella has done a bit of sightseeing, something dairy cows generally don't get to enjoy. When she was due to come back, I wondered what her reaction would be; would she remember the place where she was born and had grown up?

I needn't have worried. Until she came, I had had no reason to move the steer out of the paddock. The morning after she returned, she made it clear by her behaviour—if she were a dog I would have said she had some pointer in her—that the time had come to open a more suitable grazing area. She even remembered which pasture she had been in before she left last fall.

And so, the evening after I had opened the orchard pasture to her, it was clear I would have to remind her that it was milking time. I had walked around to the orchard field often enough in summers past, but this time was especially sweet because it had seemed, only a year ago, that I would not be getting any more cows.

Going out the door into the paddock at the opposite side of the barn from the house was like walking into another world. Between dusk and dark the trees at the edge of the paddock were black and two-dimensional. The water in the watering trough, stirred by a light breeze, looked like liquid steel as it picked up light from a sky, which did not have much light to give. From the woods beyond the trees came sleepy bird songs, the natural world's *Nunc dimittis*, disembodied but distinct in the general hush of nightfall.

Ahead was the cows' path, a narrow line of darkness in the almost colourless grass. It curves around the big bridge timbers we had discovered at the dump and hauled home many years ago. I forget what plan we had for them. Now they are little more than hummocks in the grass, but the cows still remember they are there and give them a wide berth.

Above the timbers, between the barn and the granary, the paddock rises slightly then slopes away toward the stream that flows both behind and beside this part of the farm. Although the trees still edge one side of the field, the space here holds more light since it is no longer caught between the trees and the barn.

I made my way along the path with the cows following, listening to the sounds of the evening and enjoying the in-between quality the coming of night confers on the familiar world of the day. The hawkweed flowers that bloom in clusters there were already closed above their thin stems.

This summer, the cows have made a new path for themselves, following the fence at the upper edge of the field even though the old path I was on was still clear enough. Their new path ran above a big boulder projecting out of the ground like the shape of a heart or an upside-down map of Africa with lichens demarcating geographical features known only to imagination.

I was speculating on the reason for the new path, cows being such conservative creatures most of the time. Then I saw ahead of me, luminous in the dim light, what appeared to be a path of stars just where the old path ran; daisies had completely filled the narrow track, blooming nowhere else in this part of the field. The bright flower heads shining in the dim light and flowing with the path toward the orchard was a magical sight.

I wondered if the cows had thought so too.

Chapter 7: Come Wind, Come Weather

Fog in the holler
Brings horses to the collar.
Fog on the hill
Brings water to the mill.

New Brunswick proverb

Even as a child I loved Weather. I still remember the early December blizzard that brought our part of Pennsylvania to a standstill and closed my school for four days when I was ten. Part of the pleasure, no doubt, was a week off school coupled with the knowledge that the Christmas holidays would follow almost immediately. But a real part of my pleasure was in the storm itself. I had a sense, even then, of the natural world as not simply the passive background for human affairs but as a giant of generally peaceable mien who, nevertheless, when stirred to anger or other strong emotion, was not to be withstood.

It has always been Weather with a capital "W" that has attracted me. It serves as a reminder that there are Powers moving behind the trivial façade of what we call "ordinary life." Living on the farm taught me that all Weather has its mysteries and links us with wonders.

The rain, brought in on a south wind, started just before 6:30 this morning. In the wisps and shreds of smoky cloudwrack flung past under the heavy clouds, it was hard to tell whether the sun was up or not.

Not long after the rain began, I knelt before the big wood stove in the kitchen like one of the devout at a Shinto shrine performing another of the old familiar domestic rituals, dragging soot and fly ash out through the tiny cleanout port below the oven. Manipulating the long-handled tool provided by the manufacturer for this task, I found myself trying to imagine the structures behind the tiny opening, in the way a blind person must try to imagine the shape of a tree.

Kindling set carefully on the coals from last night's fire snapped and popped into radiant life. I shoved a couple of sticks of hardwood into the firebox before it occurred to me that with a strong south wind blowing the outside temperature hardly called for a major amount of added indoor heat. Never mind. Even with a plentiful supply of matches and lots of old newspapers with which to start a blaze going again, I still find it hard to let the fire go out once the green of summer has passed into fall shades of red, yellow, and brown.

As the fire gradually waxed hot and sure of itself, I noted with satisfaction that cleaning out the ash underneath the oven had had the desired effect, no smoke curled up around the edges of the cast iron lids on the cooking surface, as it had been doing for the last several weeks. A few minutes later I shut the damper and the door below the firebox and turned to other chores. As I did so, I listened to the quiet *sursum corda* of the fire beginning to radiate heat into the room and the kettle beginning to hum its high-pitched hymn to hot water.

By the time I came up from the barn after the morning chores, the rain had stopped and the sky, which earlier had seemed only a foot or two above the chimney, had risen off the hill behind the farm. Though no less dark on the whole, the sky now showed brightish patches here and there, which hinted of more day yet to dawn.

Our weather vane is getting old. It no longer bothers to report every little puff from this direction or that, preferring to wait for a significant stir, the sort of lapse that someone is sure to notice and wonder about. Most of the time it just sits there pointing west since that is where most of our wind comes from around here. But it certainly knows about this southerly wind, and, now, as I step up onto the side porch, it is veering between west and northwest as though it thinks it might be investigated for dereliction of duty.

Did the wind all of a sudden stop blowing from the south and start blowing from the northwest? Or did it sweep around in a majestic arc from south to southeast and so on through the compass points to stop at northwest? Or go the other way? From the way it blew my barn door open I would judge it must have swung around through west to northwest.

A nature writer whose eyes are obviously a good deal better than mine suggests that we should really be able to see the wind, by training our eyes to look for the fine bits of chaff and insects being swept along in the flow. I wish him the best of luck, but I prefer to look for the big signs like the way the trees toss their branches and the direction the weather vane is pointing.

Now, in the early afternoon, the sun is bright in a pale blue sky and the wind continues to toss the trees from the northwest. It's almost as warm now as it was in the early dawn. The kitchen fire has gone to coals again but I'll not let it go out. "October's bright blue weather" is upon us, and when the sun goes down the temperature will drop like a stone and likely give us our long expected frost.

It's time to stroll out to the garden and pick the rest of the tomatoes.

One of the first things I did after we had moved from the city to this farm was to start keeping a daily record of the weather and its vagaries. I chose to start keeping records in a Pocket Planning Guide & Country Calendar I had picked up along the way. My first entry was Tuesday, July 12th: "Arrived about 10 o'clock in evening. Unloaded both cars and roof of the van before rain that had threatened for three hundred kilometres began to fall." By the end of that year entries began to gather a semblance of order. For December 31st I read: "Clear, beautiful. 22 degrees F at 7 p.m."

The Weather Journals were not only places for observations about the natural world, but a place to record memorable family events as well. For example, on Wednesday, September 7th there's a brief note: "School starts;" On the 10th, just two months after we arrived, I wrote, "Bought a Jersey cow for $225." Looking back now, I can see that, although we hadn't yet admitted it to ourselves, buying that cow was an indication we were settling in to stay. In the next year's book I see that we purchased our second Jersey cow on August 14th. I also noted that was the year we needed a well drilled. The original dug well had nearly gone dry in that summer's drought.

Weather began to be an important element in our wellbeing. It became something to pay close attention to and not just a matter of "should I take a raincoat or not?" November 20th to 23rd gets a note in the second year's Journal as well. "Coldest weather at that time of year in 100 years." We would know plenty of cold weather in the years to come, living as we do, halfway between the equator and the North Pole.

And here too, is the first indication we were working out the growing season for the garden, recorded as May 7th to September 14th that year. Looking at the entries for September 13th, I can see now what I couldn't see then, the signs of frost approaching. I had found and put up my father's barometer by then and began recording morning and evening readings. On the evening of September13th, the barometer had risen above thirty inches of mercury for the first time since early August, and the sky was clear with a northerly wind. Now, some twenty years later, a rapidly rising barometer, a clear sky, and a light wind from anywhere except the south, any time from early September on, sends us running for old bed sheets to cover the tomatoes and squash.

I don't remember who gave me my first bit of local weather-lore about "fog in the holler." With the Millstream Valley before us and Gibbon Mountain behind us, we do pay attention to the morning dew and damps. Fog in the valley in the morning is generally a sign of a fine day to come, the sort of day that fifty years ago would have the horses harnessed up and ready for the day's work in the fields. A fog hanging on Gibbon Mountain, however, indicates a day inclined to be wet. Though water no longer turns any of the seven mills that once graced Millstream, summer rains still makes glad the summer fields and gardens hereabouts.

As the fall season lengthens, the garden harvest is in, and we move toward winter, the Weather signs are less clear.

When the lilacs and the apple trees have lost their leaves, one has the feeling that the summer's sand has run through the hourglass and nothing remains in the bulb above but a faint shimmer of dust. Nothing for it at this time but to gird up the loins and try to remember where we put the snow shovels way back in the greening of the year.

"Breathes there the man with soul so dead, who never to himself hath said ..." what a great blizzard!

Well, enough of Sir Walter Scott, who didn't exactly say it that way, but I'm sure he would have if he'd had the chance, aware as he was of the way grand moments in Nature's realm alter our perception of ourselves and of our surroundings.

A road grader in its snowplough manifestation went down our road a day after the snow started. It had the look of a machine that has been heavily put upon. Not only did it sound like a small airplane in distress, causing me to look for the insurance papers for the house, but when it went past it behaved as if it knew that by the time it reached the turn no one would know a plough had been by.

In case you're wondering, I do know one mustn't rejoice in things like blizzards. For one thing, all the tellers at my local counting house and overdraught recording society look upon anything other than bright warm weather as a personal affront. I know, because I have rashly exulted in a good soaking rain that came over the hill in time to save a young garden from extinction and been greeted by stark disbelief on the part of one or t'other of 'em. I had the distinct feeling that my credit rating had just sunk another notch. Imagine the effect if I were to zoom in rejoicing in a blizzard!

But faugh, say I, and pshaw; when one is snug as a bug in a rug and is able to enjoy the weather without having to enter into an adversarial relationship with Nature, a little revelry with the old girl in one of her grander moods is surely a harmless pastime that treads on no one's toes.

My cousin Bill and I, as younkers, were great celebrators of thunderstorms. I remember one grand occasion when we were literally chased out of a field by a rather testy little line storm intent on frying our hides before we could get the last load of hay away to the safety of the mow. Even Bill and I found all this atmospheric attention a bit excessive. The horses didn't seem too fussy about waiting around to observe the details either. But it was a great storm, especially since the horses, the hay, and we all survived. It remains in the memory to this day.

This last blizzard, aside from the fact that it came on a weekend, limiting its usefulness as a means of avoiding work, was a real corker. It was the sort of storm that makes me take down a copy of John Greenleaf Whittier's *Snowbound* and read it again. Whittier clearly was another blizzard-buff. If we have to live up here in the frozen arctic, we might as well have some storms to talk about for the benefit of those more salubriously located who believe it's only because of governmental hocus-pocus that the glaciers are kept back out of sight of the Trans-Canada Highway. These are the same people who believe the tides in the Bay of Fundy are turned off after Labour Day.

This past Saturday morning, when I drove one of the children into town to catch the early train, the snowfall already had a determined look about it. I got back to the farm just in time to help load our heifer onto a truck for her trip to her new home. By the time our neighbour came with his tractor and pulled the truck out of the snowbank into which it had slid on its trip down the driveway, we were really descending to particulars, egged on by a perfectly poisonous east wind. Having made sure both cars were at the top of the driveway where blowing and drifting snow was bound to maroon them even if the storm petered out, I was free to retreat to the house and putter around. I was now secure in the knowledge there was no possible way I could get to town, no matter how badly we needed whatever it would be that we would be sure to need before the day was out.

On Sunday afternoon, in the deepening dusk, Alice and I put on snowshoes and walked down over the fields, accompanied by a sliver of a new moon and the remaining cloud-scud, tinted purple in the sunset. We both fell over more than once with laughter greeting laughter. The dogs, who insisted on coming with us, would not have made the cast for *Nanook of the North*.

As the trees lost their solidity and turned into black paper silhouettes against the luminous blue-black of the sky, we came back to the warmth of lights in the windows of the house. In the barn, a multitude of creatures were waiting for their evening care. What a warm, precious world! What a good world, at that! Without the blizzard, we would have taken it all for granted.

It all started when we came down here to stay. There was a country store type thermometer hanging on the little kitchen porch and I had my father's old barometer to hang up inside. What could have been more inevitable than to begin to keep track of the temperature and barometric pressure in a gardener's calendar with a view to being able to tell when it was time to do whatever we needed to do, like plant beans or pick the tomatoes?

The first summer we were here, a long series of days with temperatures in the nineties F gave me joy, having always preferred heat to cold. Many years in Toronto, where it was perfectly possible to have really hot weather at Easter and chilly weather the rest of the summer, made us long for a place, where summer meant something more than long sleeves and sweaters.

Temperatures like those of our first summer have never returned in quite the same startling way. I rather suspect that old thermometer had something to do with it. Hanging where it did, facing into the southwest, it was perfectly sited to report enthusiastically on the effect of direct sunlight on white clapboards.

The next year I put the thermometer in the woodshed. In that location, the sun was no longer a problem but the shaded space was. Unlike the year before, when the heat had been so prominent in our record keeping, now a distinct chill crept into our readings, even on what otherwise seemed to be hot days in mid-summer.

By the time the next summer rolled around, we had done a bit of construction and now had a new porch on the back of the house, facing northwest rather than southwest. To accompany the new porch, we had a new thermometer, one that would tell the current temperature but would also remember the day's high and low. I mounted the new thermometer facing in rather than out on one of the porch pillars so it wouldn't catch the late afternoon sun.

I think it was the next winter that I first got carried away by statistics. Looking back over the records from the previous year, I saw that by February the average temperature, while cold, was beginning to move gradually upwards. The previous February, with a house full of active youngsters, we had learned a new term—cabin fever. With February coming round again I thought I could calm the fever pitch amongst the young. As a benign scientific guru, I began a chart on which we could all see the advance of the average temperature from week to week, even if we couldn't feel it.

On the last day in January, a thaw that had begun a week before still held sway. Exposed ground showed grass greening up and the daytime high temperature well above freezing. I got out a piece of graph paper, numbered the days in February across the bottom, and the degrees up the side, allowing for the possibility that the daily average temperature might occasionally fall back below zero. When I wrote up the day's events that night, I casually noted that the evening temperature, for the first time in a week, had crept below zero.

As it turned out, that was the coldest February in these parts for the past century. A fierce northwest wind blew for two weeks. The weather was so cold that the dirt floor in the root cellar froze all the way to the middle. It was so cold the water pipes to the kitchen sink froze, which was the only water we had. It was so cold I had to add another piece of graph paper below the original one to track the dismal record. It was enough to depress a polar bear. Needless to say, the chart eventually started an upturn, but by then nobody was watching.

As the years went along and the records kept accumulating, I thought I could say, within two standard deviations, when the last frost in the spring was likely to menace our garden and when the approach of the first frost in the fall made tomato picking advisable. Statistics were once again exercising their hypnotic fascination.

I announced, in the measured tones of one secure in impeccable statistics, that once past the first week in March the daytime high would be consistently above freezing. Blessed thought, and well before the first day of spring. All went just as predicted until the middle of March, at which point the mercury in the thermometer congealed and all pretence of warm days vanished. The warm days eventually came back, but my standing, as an oracle, has never recovered.

My mother would often say, "When are you going to clean up that mess in your room?" I prefer the term "chaos" myself, partly because all the top brains in any branch of science you care to mention are happily churning out papers on chaos-theory. It has taken them a long time to catch up with what was standard operating procedure around the farm.

For the first time, I was looking forward to hurricane season this year. Not, I hasten to add, because I was hoping to experience one but because I thought a hurricane might do us some good, as, in retrospect, seems to have happened.

Only gradually is humanity beginning to recognise how intimately the elements of our earthly existence are tied together, how a small event here can cause a major event somewhere else, how the warmth of a part of the Pacific Ocean can affect the weather over much of North America. Scientists call it "sensitive dependence on initial conditions." The investigation of these relationships has generated a whole new realm of science, sometimes called "non-linear physics," or "chaos studies."

Chaos turns out to have a lot more to do with our world than we might want to think, although I suspect most of us, if pressed, could identify a lot of chaos pretty close to home. Now, however, as scientific studies look more and more closely at chaotic systems like the turbulence of a swift stream flowing around rocks in a stream-bed, or the behaviour of the stock market, or the weather from day to day, we are struck by the fact that every element of the whole physical world is influenced by every other element in the physical world in ways we can never hope to define.

For example, a butterfly flitting from one bush to the next in Australia can set in motion perturbations in the atmosphere that may culminate in huge storms in North America. Who knows what damage the slamming of a door might do? In a world that longs for peace, what is the effect of a single word spoken in anger?

This past summer, it seemed as if one could almost grasp the connectedness of things as day after day passed without rain, the ground grew drier, and grass stopped growing and began to take on a metallic sheen. When clouds gathered overhead they hung there almost without motion and then vanished like figures in a dream. It seemed that heaven and earth had suffered a divorce. As the earth grew drier it lost its attractiveness to the sky and all communication between them was cut off. It was hard to imagine what might serve to renew the bond.

It's a strange thought—the idea of drought in a part of the country that's covered with so much water. Streams and rivers and lakes and wetlands and the great Bay of Fundy, with its huge volume of water sloshing back and forth with the pull of the moon, are such dominant realities. How can we possibly lack for an element that surrounds us in such abundance? And yet—strange but true—although the water continued to flow in the majestic Saint John River and the tides continued to draw huge quantities of water from the ocean into the Bay of Fundy, the little brook that runs through our property drew away from its normal banks and in some places disappeared entirely. Our pond, which has held its level through every dry spell we have had up to this year, shrank lower and lower until it looked as though it might vanish entirely.

There was still water overhead, or so it seemed, as cloudy day succeeded cloudy day in the last part of July. Our part of the world seemed to be holding its breath, hoping for rain, but the clouds granted no such blessing. And still the land held its breath. The barometer, which around here usually bounces up and down with great abandon, hardly moved for days at a time. When it did move, it was only a fraction of an inch. The wind, too, which always seems to be moving on this hillside, lowered to a whisper and sometimes died entirely. The sun came out and seemed set to stay.

What could end the spell we seemed to be under? What butterfly somewhere in the world was going to shimmer just the right way to set up a tiny breeze which would grow into a mighty wind that could sweep away air that had become cobwebby and stagnant and, finally, give us a breath of life?

In a chaotic system it's impossible to trace effect back to cause, to point out the very butterfly, but, finally, the mighty wind that roared toward the coast of North Carolina was easy enough to spot as the hurricane. It bounced off Cape Hatteras and then angled up the Atlantic seacoast without coming ashore. But it has been the broom we needed to sweep away the cobwebs. The barometer is moving again. Wind and rain have returned. Has the spell at last been broken? Time alone will tell.

Sometimes winter storms are wonderful things. We would listen carefully to the radio to find out if the weather forecast had been upgraded from "Winter Storm Advisory" to "Heavy Snowfall Warning" and if it mentioned things like northeast winds with strong gusts. The clock radio would come on promptly at 6 a.m. In the half-light, we would speculate whether Alice, a teacher at the local high school twelve miles away, would need to go to work. Often, on those days, luck was with us and without having to wake up entirely we would hear the announcement that schools in District Four were closed. We would turn off the radio and settle down for the rare luxury of extra sleep on a workday morning.

Alice woke me during this morning's storm with the news that there was no water. My ears told me the weatherman had not been speaking idly when he predicted high winds from the east. My eyes, looking through the window at a nearly opaque greyness in which even nearby trees bore no more than dark grey suggestions of branches, confirmed the "Heavy Snowfall Warning."

Life during a storm like this tends to gravitate toward the wood stoves that are our source of heat. Dogs and cats abandon their various private dwelling spaces and relocate near the warmth of the stoves. Even our part Newfoundland, who prefers to sleep outside under the porch even on the most frigid nights, became a hazard to navigation this morning by flopping down in a loose sprawl in front of the big cast iron kitchen stove. He had a point. Alice and I relocated from the chilly dining room to the kitchen table for our breakfast in pleasant proximity to the stove with its delicious supply of radiant heat.

A quick check after breakfast showed no improvement in the water supply. Resigned to dungeon duty, I went out to the breezeway to gather up the propane torch and then descended into the cellar with its thick dry-stone walls and dirt floor.

When we moved to this old farm seventeen years ago, we left behind a lot of what we had been taught to think of as basic conveniences of modern life. When we arrived here, the plumbing consisted of cold water from a dug well pumped to a recently installed sink in the kitchen. Hot water was produced for specific purposes via a kettle on the kitchen stove.

One of our first purchases was a tin tub of elegant design to place beside the wood stove for bathing. The antique dealer from whom we bought it was amused to hear how we intended to use it. He had just sold another one like it to the Provincial Museum.

My Christmas present to the family that first winter was an excursion into the mysteries of plumbing. The kitchen range came with one side of the firebox looking rather like an old, flattened cast iron radiator. With a cold-water lead-in and a tank behind the stove into which hot water would move by convection, we then had what we recognized as true luxury—hot water on tap.

In the course of creating this wonder, I spent a good deal of time in the aptly named cold cellar contemplating the obscure details of what is called a "shallow-well pump." How well I remember the laconic words of my friendly plumbing supply dealer when I called to report that the pump was running but there was no water upstairs. "Sounds like she's lost her prime," he offered. I got to know the symptom well.

I've never been one of those who seem to intuitively understand the inner life of machinery. Water pumps seem to me more mysterious than most other mechanical devices. All I knew was that if the pump had "lost her prime" it meant I would have to spend time in the darkest, dankest corner of our cellar pouring water from a teapot with a broken spout into a ridiculously small opening on the pump while listening for the change in the sound the pump makes when "she catches her prime."

It was hard to explain to friends, who depended on city water supplies, with how much hope one listens for the change in the whirring noise the pump makes when "she catches her prime," or the gloom that settled on me when the baritone burble faded—yet again—into a dry soprano. Teapot after teapot of water would be emptied in a vain effort to placate the vile tempered machine while my mood grew darker and darker and thoughts that would have pleased a Luddite chased themselves around in my head. Suddenly, however, for no reason that could be determined, the baritone burble would be prolonged and water could be heard exiting the pump and splashing into the pressure tank beside it.

There was no victory celebration on these occasions. I had no idea why the water began to flow. Thoroughly chilled, I would put the teapot down amidst the cobwebs and the condensation, ready for next time, and head back upstairs glad to put the water supply out of my mind for a while anyway.

This time, however, the pump was not at fault. Somewhere in the pipes that ran between the cellar and the upstairs there was a clot of ice. When the cold is intense, as it is today, the cold stones of the cellar walls suck any heat out of the cellar the way a sponge sucks up water. I know the water pipes run close to the walls at various places, but I hoped the trouble this time was where it was last time, close to the pressure tank, where a quick blast of heat from the propane torch would solve the problem.

Half an hour later I had to admit that Jack Frost was smarter than I thought. Water was getting to the tank all right. The problem could be anywhere in what now seemed to be miles of water pipe that ran through the cellar and disappeared upstairs. As I cautiously ran the torch along one pipe, which was secured to the wooden floor joists over my head, I thought how ironic it would be if in the process of attempting to thaw the pipe I set fire to the house.

After another half hour of carefully heating pipes without success, I was, as the Psalmist says, "at my wit's end." Then, for some reason, my eye fell on an elbow of pipe tucked away in the dark southeast corner of the basement. Thinking of the wind roaring in the tops of the trees outside, I reached up into the corner and was met with a sharp blast of winter air sneaking through a tiny gap between stone foundation and wooden sill right where the elbow was located.

With fingers crossed, I plied the torch and, oh joy!, a crackling noise and then a rush of water through the pipe. I did not require it, but I got a hearty confirmation when Alice shouted, "The water's running!" It was then the work of only a moment to fit a bit of insulation between the pipe and the wall. Dungeon duty, at least for now, was done.

By this time, the stoves I had lit before breakfast were burning steadily and the heat of summers long past had chased winter's chill into out-of-the-way corners. "It's a good thing we put all that wood in on Saturday," Alice remarked as I fed another stick of wooden sunshine into a stove. "It is indeed," I agreed and, with the fires made up again, I settled down in the living room with a book and a virtuous sense of duty well done.

Let the wind roar a tigerish noise in the poplar trees beside the house. Let millions of tiny snowflakes whisper urgently to us as the wind dashes them against the windows. Winter is not an abstraction here in the country. Seventeen years earlier, we had chosen to leave the city and the separation cities engender from the created order of the world, from wind and weather, from our place in the whole of Creation. We don't regret that for a minute, even if the pipes do freeze on occasion. Besides, a good storm gives us a much-appreciated day off.

I have often had occasion to brood, moodily, on Christina Rossetti's little jewel of a Christmas poem, "In the Bleak Midwinter," which begins,

In the bleak midwinter, frosty wind made moan,
Earth stood hard as iron, water like a stone;

I mention this because, as much as I admire the poem, I frankly don't know what she was thinking about when she wrote those lines. She was born in London, after all. We survived a winter in England in the midst of a coal strike. There may have been a bit of ice here and there, and some snow now and then, but nothing like the dooryard of Frankenstein's castle that we are presently experiencing.

Furthermore, the poet goes on to tell us that "Snow had fallen, snow on snow, snow on snow," but if there was a lot snow all over the place it stands to reason the ground wasn't frozen. Maybe she hadn't gotten out her snow shovel yet. Maybe someone else did snow shovelling for the Rossettis. Whatever the case, she certainly was not living in the True North strong and frozen.

Around here it can be worth your life to step off the porch in winter. Even the four-footed beasts are getting into trouble. A while back our young dog rediscovered his shoe. Now, this shoe should be in a museum where its durability could be properly appreciated. Alice originally gave him the shoe when he was just a feckless pup a few weeks old. Now, nine months later, the shoe is much the same, and Baggins is just as feckless as ever. In his case, maturation seems to have been laid aside in what were deemed non-vital areas of brain development.

Anyway, we had tied this shoe by its shoelace to a nail on the skirt of the old kitchen table where Baggins would do Tarzan of the Apes rushes at it, gleefully swinging round with it when the shoelace brought him up short. There came a day when revelry of this sort became a serious hazard, especially when the table began to join in the fun by threatening to relocate, after a particularly exuberant whee-hah. The shoe was banished to the out-of-doors.

After the first snowfall, Baggins lost his shoe in a drift somewhere. A Baggins without his shoe was far worse that a Baggins with his shoe. When he had his shoe, we could pretend to have an interest in getting it away from him, thus ensuring that he kept a respectful distance whilst shaking the poor shoe as though illustrating the old threat, "I'm going to shake you till your teeth rattle."

Fortunately for the dog, a delightful rain in mid-December did an excellent job of melting all the snow. Baggins found his shoe, although he doesn't remember where. He brought it up to the porch with him that evening when it was time for him to come in. The temperature was sub-tropical at that point and the rain was still being delivered in quantities that suggested a big water main somewhere up in the firmament needed immediate attention.

However, to the benefit of the oil companies, someone turned down the thermostat before repairing the water main, and, alas, the next morning our poor dog found his shoe "welded" firmly to the porch floor. In fact, the freezing rain had glazed the whole scene with a couple of inches of glare ice, which, in turn, bolstered the sagging fortunes of the Plaster of Paris magnates, whose sales to hospital emergency wards had been falling off. The cheery northwest wind then roared in helping people who had fallen down slide in a southeast direction while freezing any bits of unprotected anatomy. The temperature then plummeted on the northwest wind and wood, oil, propane, and electricity were fed virtually non-stop into the maws of any operable heat source throughout the community.

It has been literally downhill all the way since then. Downhill, because there is no earthly method of getting back up whatever hill it is you just slid down. Our driveway is so smooth it would make a furniture refinisher weep.

One good thing, though, Baggins finally pried his shoe loose. Now, if you can get to it and give it a heave downhill, it takes a long time for the shoe and dog to stop sliding, which gives me time to crawl on hands and knees back to the house with the milk pail handle between my teeth.

The weather of late winter and early spring in New Brunswick is different than the weather I remember from my childhood in southern Pennsylvania. It took quite a while after moving north before I could bear a late and brief spring that turned almost at once into a hectic summer. My springs in Pennsylvania were long and luxurious, moving with elaborate and gradual ceremony into the heat of summer. Fall was pleasant too, but not as special as the season around the spring equinox. Here, in the north, the emphasis is reversed. spring does indeed "come slowly up this way," but it is the coming and not the spring itself that is slow.

"Mud season" was a term that had not entered our vocabulary until we moved to the farm. The road leading to the farm remained unpaved for the first ten years after our move, and each spring we became intimately familiar with mud season. Winter in a city in a northern climate can be unpleasant, with its dirty snow and floes of black ice that slowly creep out from the gutters toward the centre of the street, but the beginning of the great thaw in the northern countryside produces an effect in its own way more impressive.

As the frost begins to come out of the ground, the upper layers of soil, now water-soaked, yet rest upon the frozen subsoil. Boots are an essential for getting from house to barn but boots for cars haven't been invented. Drive a car or two or three over thawing ground and the reality of mud season quickly becomes apparent.

It's raining again today, provoking a neighbour to remark, in careful subjunctives, that he thought if there was much more rain it might be a bit too much. Country people are always cautious about making out-and-out judgements about the natural world and its behaviour.

Spring seems to be doing a dance of the seven veils. It's been a good maple sap run and there have been days when the high was above 50 F, but there was also a night not long ago when the low was 10 F. We've had snow, some, and rain, a lot. We've taken to parking half way down the driveway because the upper reaches are a reasonable facsimile of the "Slough of Despond." As John Bunyan wrote in *Pilgrim's Progress*, "Here, therefore, they wallowed for a time, being grievously bedaubed with dirt."

As mud season advanced, we first took the car up the outside of the driveway and then, as the ruts deepened that way, up the inside of the driveway, searching for the "high ground" that politicians also seek but rarely find. Our search was eventually likewise in vain because no matter what the outer set of wheels might be doing, the inner set had to run in the mud we were trying to avoid. Right now, most of the upper part of the driveway looks a lot like what I imagine the Oregon Trail must have looked

"…the chickens have a splendid time roaming…
and commenting as they go…"

like after the first thousand or so Conestoga wagons had passed by in the spring.

The livestock is getting out now and then when the weather is pleasant. It didn't take this lot of chickens long to find out what we were feeding the wild birds, and where. Fortunately, they have been content to scour the ground, so the regular clientele is not totally deprived of nourishment in the feeders above.

I feel sorry for the juncos and their friends who prefer to find their food on the ground, but short of putting up chicken wire there is not much I can do, and the chickens do have a splendid time, roaming over the place and commenting as they go about all the wonders they find. They have had a grand time in the orchard, cleaning up all the windfall apples languishing from last fall, not to mention associated slugs and bugs. Apple mush is not my idea of a delicacy, but there's no disputing about tastes.

Sir Francis Drake, the Noble Duck, and his truly fair, New Sue, seem content with the puddles in the driveway and have not yet gone down to check out the still frozen pond. The other evening I drove out of the yard about dusk and passed Sir Francis sitting at the entrance to the chicken house. New Sue and the chickens had all retired for the night leaving Sir Francis to enjoy what was left of the evening. He had the look, I thought, of a duck who thought things were quite tickety-boo.

The cows, too, go out now to stand around in the paddock, tidying each other up with their tongues. Maggie spent quite a long time the other day, licking her daughter's neck, which she evidently found needed cleaning. I was glad to see this hint of the maternal instinct since, in the barn, Maggie's strategy seems to be to brain her, if she can.

The dogs spend their newfound days outdoors pursuing some sort of scam. They drift off in an elaborately casual way in the direction of a neighbouring German Shepherd's house and return a while later pleased as punch with bones they have obviously snitched. They spend the rest of the day acquiring a fine coat of mud, which, by some reversal of polarity only dimly envisaged by science, they immediately deposit on floors and surroundings as soon as they come in.

The most interesting natural phenomena of the season is the eruption of a spring part way down the driveway. It has put out a goodly flow of water, cutting a nice channel for itself down the driveway and then onto the road where it fans out into a delta about two car lengths wide. The headwaters of this junior Mississippi springs from the ground on the high side of the driveway about a foot from the ditch intended to carry water safely away from the drive. The bottom of the ditch is maybe a foot and a half lower than the driveway at that point, so I figure the water must be diving down below the ditch in order to come up on the drive. There's just no arguing with some folks.

Our neighbour's right. A bit more rain might be a bit too much.

Inside the farmhouse, our activities changed to suit those neither-here-nor-there seasons such as late summer or early spring. It being a farmhouse of some antiquity, we learned to listen to advice from old sailing masters when a wind howled around us. In a clipper or a man-of-war, the wind determines how the sails are to be set. At the farm, a strong wind coming from the east meant that some of the warmth inside would be pushed into the western corners, while a western wind had the opposite effect. Rather than trim sails we did not have, we would feed the stoves instead.

The blustering wind was in the southwest all of yesterday and was still blowing strong this morning when we got up. During the night the temperature rose higher than it had been in the evening when I checked it before we went to bed. Then the wind, threatening to make sleep a sporadic affair, whistled in our bedroom window, until I closed and locked it against the intrusion.

Now, in the early afternoon of the next day, the wind has gone around into the northwest and the temperature is falling fast enough that at lunchtime I went out to gather up an armful of wood to start a fire in the kitchen stove. The house is dark, and showers of rain spattered the windows most of the morning. The cows are in their stanchions for the day, the first time in a long time.

There is something mournful and melancholy about some of the winds we get around here, and yesterday's wind could be Exhibit A. The original framers placed this house so carefully that it generally welcomes a wind coming down the valley from the west but makes it hard for an east wind to get a good grip. When we arrived, there were only three windows on the long east wall and one of those, in the kitchen, is only about the size of the average cellar window.

In the winter, high winds from any direction use the big poplars between the house and the barn the way a musician uses a tuning fork, only it is not necessary to put your ear close to the trees to get the pitch. Periodically, the roar is enough to make a person throw the bedclothes over his head and think of the advantages of hibernation as a way of coping with winter.

Sometimes in the middle of the night, I'll wake and hear a blast of wind from far away hurling itself against the trees in the woods, sweeping towards us, nearer and nearer until, with a roar, it sets the poplars to quivering and bids fair to lift the corner of the house right off the foundation.

Even in the summer there is a wind that puts my nerves on edge. I've never quite figured out exactly where it comes from, but I know it well. It seems to be a west wind like any other west wind, except that it gets into the kitchen and scatters papers and anything else moveable it can find into distant corners and under furniture.

The kitchen door stands open most of the summer, letting the screen door do duty against insects, but when this particular half-a-gale comes to the door looking for handouts there is nothing to do but shut both doors firmly until it goes away to bother someone else. I suspect it is the same wind that, in the days when we put our own hay in the mow, used to delight in rolling the loose hay backwards down the hay loader until it produced a fine tangle.

This morning, the blustery wind—bluster that might have been taken for enthusiasm and energy—only served to dull the spirit and hunch the shoulders of those who had to be out in it. On any other morning I would have left the big door to the paddock open after the cows came in as a sort of sign to them that they could depart again as soon as the milking was done. Not this morning. None of us was enthusiastic about going out again.

As if the commotion in the air was not enough to afflict a person, a rain squall sent water pouring from the edge of the roof, a goodly amount of which got me in the neck, both at my going out and my coming in the barn door.

Well, let the melancholy days come as come they will. Here in the country we can always console ourselves that there is more water for the wells to draw on next March, and dull weather makes the colours in the trees seem brighter. A wind like the one we had yesterday makes fair weather all the more welcome when it comes.

If wind and sky were always fair
The sailor would not watch the stars,
And David's Psalms had ne'er been sung
If grief his heart had never wrung.

Benjamin Schmolk
Early 18th century German pastor and hymn writer

Hunkered down as we were among the rolling hills, our vision was limited by the height of land behind us and the ridge-lines of the landscape across the valley. Our view of the sky was likewise limited, so sometimes as we drove over a line of hills into the next valley it almost seemed as though we drove into a new sky as well.

Many times I have driven out of Sussex on my way home and felt as though each trough in the landscape was cherishing its own unique weather: broken cloud and blue sky here, dark grey alternating with light grey clouds there, and then, over Sharp's Hill into our own valley to find the clouds illuminated with wonderful sunburst effects which weren't even hinted at on the other side of the hill.

I have travelled on the prairies and felt a sense of being a bug beneath a huge glass dome. It seems you can travel forever, and the huge sky is still above you, still as it was when you set out. "Awesome" is an overworked word these days, but it accurately evokes the sensation one has when travelling on the prairies and a summer storm is "making up" somewhere overhead.

Around here it is not so. The sky has a domestic quality about it. If there are big things being planned up there, we are rarely aware of them until they surmount the hills that make our horizon. The loss of scale, however, is compensated for by a gain in familiarity which enables us to think of what is overhead as "our sky" in a way no one would think of doing when referring to the big sky of the prairies.

A while back, an article in Canada's glossy back-to-the-land periodical for business tycoons and Bay Street lawyers purported to teach weather prediction by learning about four different cloud patterns. I confess I didn't give the article much attention, but it reminded me yet again, in spite of evidence to the contrary, that I have learned some things since moving to New Brunswick.

Our first impetus toward weather prediction came from trying to figure out when to cut hay so it wouldn't get rained on. I learned a lot about cloud patterns then, everything from mare's tails to cumulonimbus, and still the hay got rained on, at least some of the time. There was one field just below the barn that had the best hay on the place, and I sometimes felt that the weather was just sitting up on the crest of the hill watching what was going on. We could cut the hay on that field on a clear day with nary a cloud in the sky and we would be lucky to get out of the field before big black rain clouds were rolled into position overhead.

My son cut that field this summer and waited a week before he brought the hay in and it never did get rained on. I thought maybe the jinx had been broken, but then realized the reason the hay had been left for a week before being gathered in was that the humidity had been so high the hay was almost as green at the end of the week as it was at the beginning.

I wish anyone good luck who thinks they are going to predict the weather around here by knowing four different cloud patterns and nothing else. We finally began to pay more attention to when the neighbours were cutting hay. I suppose this is a variation on the old joke about predicting the severity of the winter by how high your neighbour builds his woodpile, but it worked about as well as anything else. It took me years to realize that real farmers get their hay rained on too. Indeed, the writer of the book of Ecclesiastes (chapter 11:4) already knew that he who watches the weather never gets his haying done.

Our personal piece of sky is full of all sorts of things to wonder at, some, like the wind and the barometric pressure, quite invisible, and others, like the clouds and the colour of the sunset, or the halo that sometimes adorns the moon, splendidly visible. On a day like today, when there has been a bit of rain, the clouds get right down almost to our level and then, when they have gotten rid of the water allocated to this valley, they rise up and go away.

But there are all kinds of clouds, and because our piece of the sky is relatively small, we can get a good look at them. We can, if the mood is upon us, even say what we think they mean. But we don't count on it.

Chapter 8:
Pigs Is Pigs

The nice little pig with the querly tail
All soft as satin and pinky pale
Is a very different thing by far
Than the lumps of iniquity big pigs are.

Nonsense rhyme found in
Handbook of Nature Study
by Anna Botsford Comstock

We kept pigs for a number of years after we settled on the farm, and we always found the association good. Our first pig, Grover by name, lived in a pen in the barn. He was such an interesting fellow that he persuaded us to keep him long after he should have been shipped. Partly, this was owing to our inexperience with loading pigs into a truck. When the day came to move him, the experience was traumatic for all concerned. Nevertheless, we continued to raise a pig or two or three every summer for a number of years, until our daughter and son-in-law took over the responsibility.

We did adopt a somewhat unorthodox method for shipping our pigs when the time came, but the unorthodoxy was tempered by its merciful calming influence on all concerned. It did mean we gained what is called "a reputation" in the surrounding countryside. But then, what are newcomers in a rural landscape for if not to give the natives something to talk and laugh about?

Some of the old farming books we read called the pig "the mortgage lifter." And no doubt it was. In the days of mixed farming, when every small farm had a few chickens and a cow or two and a variety of crops, the pig and the chicken could be relied upon to consume whatever was left over in the way of kitchen scraps, sour milk, garden thinnings, and almost anything else that would be otherwise wasted. On such a diet and with access to pasture, a bit of shade and a wallow for hot days, a pig could wax and grow fat.

The chicken is a good composter, but the pig brings enthusiasm to the job. Indeed, all our pigs, bought in the late spring after they were weaned and in the freezer by winter, brought both enthusiasm and a kind of infectious exuberance to our midst. From the time they came as weaners (newly-weaned piglets, about 30 pounds) to the time they went, at about 200 pounds, some months later, their exuberance begot an affection quite different from that accorded the cows.

The name "pig" is the very definition of excess, and yet, in our experience, the excess was always good humoured; we never knew quite what would happen or what they would think of next.

Right now, to be accurate rather than romantic, we are in the intermediate period between the "is-it-going-to-be-summer-or-isn't-it?" and the "days-are-drawing-in" seasons. The sun hasn't got so far over the yardarm that the evenings are noticeably shorter, and the immediate drop in temperature that accompanies the sunset still leaves a comfortable margin above the dark and frosty regions we will worry about in a couple of months.

The pigs are growing apace. They no longer look like little creatures that are easily discouraged or who miss (how could they possibly?) their mother. Higgledy, the little gilt, was so much smaller than Piggledy (her litter mate) that we worried she might have a hard time getting near the food trough. We needn't have worried. She quickly learned to stand in the trough so as to protect the maximum amount of food. She now tells Piggledy where he can eat and what he can eat. She may be watching his weight, but she certainly isn't watching hers.

Not having kept pigs last summer, I am now reminded of endearing and not-so-endearing porcine traits. I had almost forgotten the quick feint with the feed bucket required to get the slops in the trough. Pigs know a food bucket when they see one, and anxiety levels are high until food is in front of them. It does no good to put the dry pig chop in first. If it is pelletized, they stand on it so as to be closer to the bucket of slops and if it is ground into meal they sniff at it and blow it all over the place. In our experience, "all over the place" means all over the bucket wielder because the wind at such moments is always on shore, just the way it is when we go to the dump.

One of our girls used to take a stout broom handle with her when she took the slops to the pigs. She said she was teaching them to stand back from the trough until the food was ready. I thought this a novel, if somewhat utopian, plan, and wished her Godspeed. It worked all right in their young and impressionable days, but there is a clear point beyond which your pig is no longer young or impressionable. By then, even a stout two-by-four would probably not make much impression, and etiquette is not on their agenda.

But here we are, "poised," as Alexander Pope said, "on this isthmus of a middle state," in the season that comes between a late spring and an early frost. We declare it to be summer and we revel in it and, like the pigs, we look neither forward nor back.

Since we kept only a few pigs each summer—three at the most—we were always fascinated at the development of their personalities. In a big hog barn, it may be possible to regard all the inmates without noting the differences, but, on a small farm, pigs have a chance, like everybody else, to be themselves. There may be ill-tempered pigs, but we never had one; demanding, yes, but not ill-tempered. After all, pigs do love to eat. Nothing makes the staff of a small farm run to phone the vet quicker than a pig who has lost interest in food.

Our pigs generally lived outdoors in the summer. We used them to root up ground, which we would later incorporate into the garden. They were thus doing good work for us and having a good time doing it. But we always brought them food in the morning and evening. Pig chop was ground up grain we bought at the Co-op. The slop bucket served to moisten the chop. Slops might consist of a mix of almost anything, usually milk, water, kitchen scraps, and any other available goodies mixed in.

"The sky is falling!" One of our two pigs (the aforementioned Higgledy) had occasion to quote Chicken Little the other day, although I doubt she's read the story. It's been tough in the pig yard ever since the electric fence was installed, and the mood, even at meal times, has been akin to a gathering of stockbrokers toward the end of October. The mood of the pigs is edgy, you might say, with a lot of furtive glances over the shoulder, even at the risk (only in the pigpen I'm sure) of losing a choice tidbit to one's dinner partner. For the pigs (I don't know about stockbrokers), even standing in the trough does not, in such times, conduce to contentment.

I've been doing what I can to ease anxiety by making sure the feed trough is close to their house and well away from the dreaded wire. (As far as I can tell, the wire is dreaded but not yet clearly identified in the porcine mind as the source of the trouble. Up to present time, the occasions when they have been attacked by a nasty shock, they have backed up into the wire because they suspected some other, harmless, object, and then had their suspicions amply fulfilled by the shock.) I've even been bringing them little kickshaws outside of regular meal times, and it was while engaged, as I thought, in this humanitarian work that the sky fell on Higgledy.

It came about in this wise. The growing season had at last yielded a sufficiency of tomatoes, string beans, and potatoes, which, supplemented by a superfluity of basil from a friend, and augmented by garlic, olive oil, and egg noodles, meant that at last it was time for *Soupe au Pistou,* the culinary pinnacle of the gardening season. I was in the garden assembling the elements of this dish when the pigs, hearing activity, naturally thought of a little lunch and emerged into the yard to see what might be forthcoming.

I was maybe 15 feet from the pen, wielding a potato fork, and just in the process of defrauding a potato plant of its little collection of tubers, when they scrambled out of their house. Having the purest of intentions, as I said, I picked up a potato I had just inadvertently stabbed with the garden fork and gave it an underhand heave in their direction.

One of the secret regrets of my life is that I cannot throw a ball, underhand or overhand, curve, drop, fastball, slider, or even a spitball and come within hailing distance of the target. Forget the major leagues, I couldn't even make a sandlot team. I therefore watched the lobbed potato as it traced its lazy arc toward—I hoped—the pigpen.

Pigs do not, I think, have good eyesight. What's more, neither of these pigs showed the slightest aptitude for sports, although I think they might be in favour of legalizing anabolic steroids. There they stood, in the geographical centre of the pig yard, as far from the electric wire as they could be in all directions, leaning on each other for protection, ears and noses trained in my direction, imploring the heavens to drop down manna from on high.

All Nature (I'm sure), as well as the pigs and I, were waiting for a sign. We got it. The potato hung briefly at the top of its arc and then began its lazy descent over the remaining distance to the pig yard.

I wish Preacher Roe, the great pitcher for the Brooklyn Dodgers, could have been there. It was only a lob, but I think he would have been impressed. Still descending, and picking up speed, the potato passed over the near side of the pig yard, over the dreaded wire, over the trough, and, with an audible "bonk," hit Higgledy exactly and precisely between the eyes. That was the last I saw of the pigs for the rest of the afternoon. They stayed safely inside the pig house.

Speaking of the sky falling, rumour has it that the world has once again failed to come to an end at somebody's prediction. I gather that last Wednesday was the big day, but as far as I can tell Gabriel was otherwise engaged. This is probably the ten to the power of twenty-threeeth time that the planet has got up on its hind legs and ignored prophecy. The first time was probably in the parking lot just inside the main gates to the Garden of Eden.

I'll bet you I know when the pigpen thought the last time was.

No matter how often we brought new pigs home, they always had something to teach us. It might, for example, be a way of leaning on the pig yard gate and squealing when dinnertime had come and we were not in evidence. No one who has heard a pig get seriously into squealing has a desire to repeat the experience. Each summer's pigs did their best to teach us promptness and diligence.

Of course, a 200-pound pig leaning on a gate can be rather hard on the gate, and, if left to its own devices, might soon be coming down to the house to see what we were doing at any hour of the day or night.

We gradually got to know something of the ways of coping with pigs, both small and large. We even put them to work for us, clearing the weeds off a piece of land we wanted to incorporate into the garden. In the early years of raising pigs we had kept them behind a set of what we called "pig gates," sturdy galvanized iron affairs which we wired together in a rough approximation of a square. These gates were heavy, and once wired together no one was enthusiastic about moving them, not even the pigs.

Although we had put up some barbed wire fences to keep the cows in their pasture and out of the garden, it wasn't too long before we discovered the effectiveness of electric fencing and how easy it was to move. Gradually we began to experiment with using the same technique to contain the pigs. According to the books we read, the trouble with using an electric fence with pigs is that the fence must be quite low to be effective; however, the pigs as they are rooting about will tend to push soil up against the wire and short it out.

It may be a problem where there are many pigs in a large area. Our pig yard, however, was small, and, as we visited at least twice a day to supply food and water, we could keep an eye out for problems. In fact, once pigs have been bitten by an electric fence and correctly identify the source of the problem they are not likely to go anywhere near the nasty thing.

A year later, that discovery led us, on a clear and cloudless day totally lacking in omens or portents, to bring our weaners home to a yard without pig gates, a yard neatly limited only by the electric fence.

We have had this year's pigs for less than a week and already piggy excess has cut a swath through our attempts at an orderly existence.

After three years of putting the pigs on a patch of ground which had originally been the vegetable garden, we decided that, interesting as our porky friends might be, the aroma of pig drifting in the open windows of the house day and night was a bit much. You have heard of an indefinable smell? The one that drifted in from the pig yard was far from indefinable, especially when the wind was from the north or northeast. The wind seemed to be in that quarter a lot last summer.

The pigs were put there originally to cope with a patch of comfrey. The first summer we were here, someone we regarded as a friend at the time had given us a comfrey plant. We planted it in the centre of the vegetable bed. (We now know all too well why she was so enthusiastic about sharing her comfrey with us. Comfrey is the vegetable equivalent of a pig. I'm sure its botanical name must have "excessive" or some similar term in it somewhere.)

We forgot about the comfrey the next spring when it was time to plough. By the time we had ploughed and disced, and all the rest of it, we had distributed small pieces of comfrey root all over the whole garden. I do believe that a piece of comfrey root smaller than a pig's sense of decorum is capable of producing seventy-five pounds of comfrey leaves in something under two months even if planted in the stony places mentioned in Matthew 13:5.

In any case, our intended vegetable garden was turned—hey, presto—into a comfrey jungle. The pigs were called in to do their thing and do it they did, but the comfrey did its thing too and it took three years of pigs to finally root out the last evidence of our original plant.

So this year we moved the pig yard downwind quite a way to a piece of pasture we wanted to incorporate into the garden. The pigs could get their jollies by rooting about and we would reap the benefit of their four legged ploughing matches. Since we had good luck in the past with electric fencing as a means of pig control, we rigged up two strands of fence wire, plugged in the fencer, and went to get the weaners.

The trouble started when we deposited our two piglets in their yard. We should have remembered to draw their attention at once to the unpleasant qualities of an electric fence by getting them up to it while holding on to them, wearing rubber boots of course. That way they could draw their own conclusions. Pigs are not slow to draw conclusions if you can get their attention, and that certainly gets their attention.

As it was, we simply dumped them out of the burlap bags they had reluctantly come home in and stood back to watch as they explored their new world. Our complacency lasted for all of half a minute. That was the time it took the pair to get up, shake themselves, renew their acquaintance, and set off at great speed to find the rest of the litter, no doubt to warn them about burlap bags.

They passed through the fence doing at least twenty miles an hour, and the shock was just sufficient to convince them they were doing the right thing. Pandemonium ensued.

People, pigs, and our two dogs attempted to come to some understanding. "Come, let us reason together," we pleaded. The pigs said, "Nix on that," and were off and running in another direction. Eventually we got them penned up in the barn, but not before Pooh Bah, our very stuffy, long-haired, ginger, ex-tomcat had the fright of his life.

There he was, having just arranged himself in a patch of daisies in an elegant pose with his tail curled around his front feet and every hair in its proper place, when one of the piglets, fleeing a pursuing child, roared around the corner of the house and ran up one side of him and down the other before his nervous system could switch from contemplation of his own perfection to red alert. When last seen, he was headed for the back pasture at a most impressive speed with his tail the size of a bottlebrush.

Myself, I'm looking forward to an interesting summer.

We did figure out, finally, that the way to educate pigs about electric fencing is to do it early. A young pig is a fast learner because he is busy identifying as many sources of food as possible in as short a time as possible. Once he has got his territory figured out, education is a dead issue.

"Pigs is pigs," the fellow said. While this on the whole may be true, it scarcely does justice to a creature that, without any particular effort, seems to transform any relationship with humans into something bordering on slapstick comedy.

Take little pigs, for example. Let's face it; little pigs are crazy. If my future was the future of most pigs, and I knew that I was being called a weaner, and I also knew that down the road much of me might come to rest in little plastic cases under the heading "wieners" in the meat department of some store, I might be inclined to hysterics too.

For a number of years, we got three weaners every spring from a neighbour and set out, basically, to raise some bacon and ham. Some of the meat we keep for ourselves, the rest we sell. In a good year, we pay ourselves back for the money we spent buying food for them while they were on the hoof.

Anyway, the three little pigs have their proper yard and a fine house, built from what we had at hand.

The great design feature is a sloping roof. The pigs appreciate the slope because it means that they can spend most of the summer scratching against the projection at the back corner.

As they get larger, the scratching becomes more enthusiastic. It also becomes louder. I remember walking out into the yard one fine summer night a number of years ago and hearing a most alarming noise. It sounded like a grasshopper plague was systematically chewing its way across the countryside and was now revelling in our garden.

Grabbing the badminton racquet we reserve for pursuing cabbage moths, I rushed for the garden. (I say "pursuing" cabbage moths advisedly. A racquet is an ecologically sound method of dealing with the pest; it does no harm to the moth unless it has just had an unhappy love affair and has lost its lust for life, and it gives the wielder of the racquet a lot of healthy exercise in the out-of-doors.) I was halfway to the garden when I realized that the locust plague was in fact one of our pigs, out having a late night scratch before turning in.

When they do turn in and fall asleep, pigs snore. They really snore! Some nights you'd think there was a whole party of ne'er-do-wells overcome on their way home from the local bootlegger, sleeping it off amongst the swine. I'm just glad we sleep on the other side of the house from the pig yard.

By the time we get our pigs in the spring, the grass is usually quite high in their yard. Nothing seems to give them greater pleasure at that time than to tear around in the grass, uttering alarmed "hornks." They'll all be sleeping peacefully side by side when suddenly, with a great "hornk," one will be up and moving. For the next few minutes all one sees is grass stems waving. What one hears is a lot of deep breathing and enthusiastic "hornking" as they careen around wildly. They always remind me of that old joke; "Shoot low, sheriff, they're riding Shetland ponies."

We put the pigs where they are because we had some particularly noxious weeds and we wanted to use the area for part of the garden. They respect our feelings about the weeds, which are supposed to be excellent forage for pigs, according to the books. By the end of the summer the entire pig yard is bare earth, except for the weeds. These they have saved carefully so generations of pigs yet unborn will have something to amuse themselves with.

Then there is the electric fence. Their noses are wet, and their feet are small and sharp. The nose is poked at anything they are curious about and the sharp feet ensure good contact with the ground. As small pigs generally feel more secure when pressed close to the other small pigs they all learn quickly about the fence. I watched our latest three little pigs standing in the yard leaning on each other one day. The outside one was investigating the world around him and he finally got to the fence. He put his nose right on it. Nothing happened, to him. The piglet furthest in, however, suddenly gave an awful squeal and went tearing off into the high grass. Rural electrification, we call it.

Pigs may be pigs, but I must say, I always miss them in the fall, even after they have stopped being cute piglets and have grown up into just plain hogs. But then, there is the bacon.

Bacon of course is but one of the splendid rewards for raising pigs and putting up with their enthusiastic disinterest in all things tidy and orderly, except in the matter of housekeeping. Pigs are not dirty, contrary to popular opinion, as long as they are accorded room to arrange their living accommodations with dignity. They will quickly choose a part of their space as a toilet, though the choice is not always what the farmer might recommend, and their much-prized mud wallow is prized because they lack the ability to perspire. Their wallow enables them to keep cool on a hot day.

Borrowing a designation from the blood donor clinics, we used to say that our pigs went from being "universal recipients" in the summer to "universal donors" in the winter. The back of the kitchen fridge was remarkably bare of mouldy food while the pigs were around.

Many people advised us against naming any of our animals, on the grounds that naming them would make them into pets. The implication, we noted, was that after your pig became your pet you were stuck with it for the rest of its natural life, an uneconomic prospect, to say the least. But we felt differently, and our children, who helped with names and helped with chores, felt differently too. While they were with us, our animals were treated with kindness and attentively cared for, though we also recognised that we were not running a zoo. We were running a small farm intended largely to free us from dependence on the commercial food chain that treats animals as so many pluses and minuses in some accountant's ledger.

We all knew that our summer's pigs would wind up in our freezer, and, like PoohBah in Gilbert and Sullivan's *Mikado*, we wished them "long life—till then!"

It all began when Alice and I discovered the newfangled, water-filled, frost-protectors we had purchased from Lee Valley Tools all lying flat on the ground devoid of water. We had installed these plastic, cone-shaped, charmingly named, "walls of water" around the tomatoes and peppers. On our way to feed the pigs we had gone to the garden to admire what a few days of good hot weather had done for the mood in the corn patch. The toppled and flattened walls of water stopped us in our tracks and we wondered what had happened.

Granted, there is always a breeze up here on this hillside. Granted, too, that the breeze is sometimes known to assume enthusiastic proportions. But surely we hadn't had enough wind to upend the walls of water. Then we noticed the footprints, quite a lot of footprints. We noticed that the footprints were small and cloven. Yep, when we looked, the pigs' happy home was strangely quiet and there was a pig-sized hole in the fence just by their house.

Of course, we had been in town all day so the last time we had had a chat with them was at the morning feeding when they had been bright and shiny, as always, and full of enthusiasm. No word had been said, at that time, about plans to tour the countryside. Doubtless they had gone to seek their fortune in the wider world. Probably they had left initially to wet their whistles, the day being hot and dry and the water-filled tepees were, no doubt, a real treat, giving them not only water but a little entertainment besides.

Well, there was no sight or sound of the happy wanderers. It's amazing, really, how big a small farm can get when you have misplaced a couple of young pigs. We shouted and banged their trough and looked about for signs. Aside from the revels in the garden there were no signs. Yes, I have read *The Last of the Mohicans*, but I didn't really see myself on my hands and knees, tracking two pigs through the long grass.

Alice went off to collect the young dog whose enthusiasm for barking at anything that moves she felt might be detrimental during delicate negotiations with the pigs, and I went to the phone to survey the neighbours. When I returned none the wiser, not only were the pigs still conspicuous by their absence, I had apparently lost my wife and dog as well. A profound silence wrapped me round with a feeling of gloom and loss.

All things pass away, silence and feelings of gloom and loss among them. A volley of hysterical barking from the woods told me that one, at least, of the missing was no longer missing. A moment later a shout told me that Alice was somehow mixed up in whatever was going on in the woods. I waited to see if pigs, wife, or dog would be the first to appear. Something momentous was clearly in the works.

It was Baggins, the hysterical mutt, attached, as it turned out, to what was purchased as a "training leash," who first appeared followed closely by Alice on the other end of the leash. Baggins was fine. Alice, encouraging him to find the pigs, had been gratified when he seemed indeed to get the scent. She had followed him through the middle of a bramble patch, over a barbed wire fence, and into the woods. She was, however, wearing shorts.

Baggins did indeed find a pig, but not the kind we were looking for. The porcupine, unimpressed, took refuge in a tree, sparing Baggins a painful lesson. Alice, somewhat the worse for wear, persuaded Baggins to leave the woods by a less demanding route. Scratch the "Great Tracking Dog Finds Lost Pigs" headline.

The pigs were gone, vanished. Perhaps pig-napped? Eaten by coyotes? We adjourned to the kitchen to consider our next move. We might just as well have spared ourselves the trouble. Something, perhaps a grunt, made me look out the door. Two young pigs, quite pleased with themselves, had come to see why we had not brought them their dinner.

They seem to have spent the day reclining in the chicken house, judging by the evidence. No doubt they found the hue and cry a touching sign of our concern but they hadn't felt called to respond.

After enticing the pigs back to their yard with the food bucket and repairing the fence, all returned to what passes for normal on this hillside farm; all, that is, except for Alice's shins.

Much of the imagery associated with life in the country, whether in written or graphic form, is wistfully nostalgic. Cows grazing peacefully under a serene sky, autumn leaves, corn shocks in the fields, and a country lane curving into the distance; or else it's "the farm in winter" with smoke curling out of the chimneys and travellers being welcomed as the light fades in the west. While the nostalgia is a tribute to the sense that we have somehow lost our connection with the earth and its seasons, it neglects to take account of the startling amount of hard physical labour that was required to harvest all that corn, and to ensure there was enough food and other supplies to keep humans and animals alive and functioning through the long, dark winters.

To keep that smoke curling out of all those chimneys through the winter, firewood had to be cut in the forest a year earlier, dragged out, reduced to manageable lengths, split, and then ranked up for seasoning. And those cows peacefully grazing in that field are only there because the farmer has made sure the field is securely bounded with fences effective for stopping the cows from disappearing into the wilderness. In fact, at one time, the legal definition of a boundary fence was "horse-high, pig-tight, and bull-strong." Even on our small farm, serenity was a quality more often to be wished for than achieved.

Frankly, I had about given up on pigs until the other day. Some time has passed since there has been a porcine personality on this place worthy of more than a passing glance. Maybe the apparent lack of personality stems from the fact that we have finally got into habits that more effectively circumscribe a pig's pleasure in creativity and general hell raising. Our fences are more firmly put together, and security is generally tighter than it used to be. The last few days, though, give signs that all is not yet ho-hum in the world of pork production.

Our weaners are now about half grown and it has been time for quite a while to expand their yard, so as to get some free rototilling done. Expanding the yard means taking away the stout enclosure they presently call home and substituting an electric fence. What with one thing and another, the task of putting in a strand of electric fence remained to be done. Of course, the electric string I was planning to use (a much more supple and easily handled product than solid fence wire) was nowhere to be found.

"I'm sure that ball of string was in with the fencing stuff."

"Well, did you look on the cellar stairs? That was where it was the last time."

[Stomping exits stage right. Cellar door slams. Silence. Cellar door slams again... Stomping reenters stage right.]

"It's not there."

"You're sure it isn't there?"

"Yes."

"You're sure you looked everywhere there?"

"Yes."

"I'm sure I saw it there just the other day."

"Well it's not there."

"Well, where could it be?"

At this point, the alert reader will have noticed that the conversation is about to go round for a second time, rather in the style of that Girl Guide song, "There's a Hole in my Bucket." Fortunately, for the sanity of both parties, I remember there's a roll of electric fence wire I can use instead, and its location.

The pigs were interested, as they always are, when we are doing something around their home. They helped by chomping on the steel fence posts I was installing and trying to pull them up as fast as I could put them in. Their enthusiasm increased when I started attaching the bright yellow insulators. Those were obviously not only edible but also delicious. The most fun of all was the still somewhat springy wire. This they pushed around with their noses, chewed on it in a determined way, and lifted it off the insulators so as to roll with it in the mud. Nothing this much fun had come their way since one of the banty hens had brought her whole brood of chicks into the pig yard for a quiet snooze.

Like the Banty Affair, the Fun with Wire Scam ended abruptly. In the case of the banty, she didn't ruffle a feather or disturb the repose of her little ones as huge pigs came snuffling around. She just made it clear to the pigs that their mother was ugly, and what's more, had been sold for bacon, and that she'd bacon them if they didn't watch out. So, they watched out.

In the case of the wire, there was a piercing squeal when the fence was plugged in, and, after several more encounters of the same kind, made even more confusing by the fact that the wire was off the insulators and rolling around the yard, they retreated to their house. They did come out to eat the next morning, but they were very jumpy. If Higgledy bumped Piggledy, she would leap like a gazelle, not sure whether she had been zapped or not. They kept yanking their noses out of the swill and looking around as if something was sneaking up on them.

In the afternoon I had to drag their trough over to their front door. They were not taking chances with the nasty thing that lived out there. Last night, after getting Alice to buy a new roll of electric string in town, I found the one I had been looking for sitting in plain view on a shelf in the barn. Now we'll see how we get on with rural electrification this time.

Next to secure fences, the farmer must provide shelter for the animals under his care. We were fortunate that our place had a fine small barn for cows and horses. Its ridgepole was straight and its foundations firm. Even a violent storm (known locally as the Groundhog Day Gale) the spring after we bought the place, which blew down more than a few barns that had stood for long years, failed to do more than blow open a pair of doors that probably had not been adequately secured.

The chickens we bought at the livestock auction in Sussex had a secure chicken house. But the pigs needed to have shelter supplied too. Our first excursions into housing pigs were tentative. As we only had two or three pigs during any given year, and only kept them from late spring until sometime in the fall, they did not need elaborate accommodations. However, it quickly became clear, as the pigs grew, the accommodations needed to be strong. A 200-pound pig having a good scratch on a corner of her house can convert a rectangular structure into a trapezoid form without much effort. And what the pigs can't achieve, the winds of the following winter can be relied upon to complete.

This year's pigs certainly have minds of their own. They have strong views on a number of subjects, including fresh air in their bedroom. Their present home is the second we have built, and I think it may not survive much beyond this year's inhabitants.

The first pig house, as I recall, was a sort of lean-to structure. Indeed, it leaned all sorts of ways and, after one of the tenants perfected her back scratching technique on one of the main props, it was never the same. A high wind the next winter redistributed various bits about the countryside, and when spring arrived it was clear that repairs were out of the question.

It was then that we began to build the present pig palace. I am not sure of the exact time, but I think it was while we were in a "build it for the ages" phase. Around the same time, we built a doghouse out of rough two-by-four and three-quarter-inch particleboard. The doghouse looked like a tenement, particularly after the resident decided to redecorate and began by tearing the burlap sack we had hung across the doorway into rags and tatters.

We painted the doghouse white but somehow it only called attention to the complete lack of anything that might be called design sense. That was OK, in a way, because the dog—I speak from a genetic perspective—was pretty much lacking in design sense as well. Pluto was part Saint Bernard and part Lab and looked as though a committee had assembled him, a committee that had totally flubbed whatever possibilities were inherent in such a conjunction.

That was our first excursion into building for the ages. I think the present pig house came along while the fit was still upon us. I remember that one thing we wanted was a portable structure so we could capitalize on the rototilling abilities of the pigs who would live in it. "Happy but productive" was to be our motto in the pig business.

The doghouse had been built pretty much freehand and looked it. The pig house was built to a design that we had found somewhere, maybe in a book. Somehow, in the process of nailing together a lot of rough two-by-six to make the base of the pig house, we forgot that the much smaller doghouse, framed with two-by-fours, was so heavy human hands could scarcely move it.

By the time the pig palace was complete, portability was strictly a matter of grim determination, stout chains, and the traction of the ex-army truck we were then using in place of the tractor we didn't have. The building did have an unforeseen ability, however. As it was dragged cross-country to a suitable location, it bulldozed any irregularities in the surface, throwing up a bow wave of dirt ahead of itself. In spite of this, when the pig palace would finally get to where we wanted it, it seemed always to be up in the air on one corner or otherwise in someway off-kilter.

Not only was it weighty, it was huge. Two or three little pigs could travel for a day and only get to the back corner, or so it seemed. Naturally, they assumed the space was for indoor facilities and used the back corner for their toilet. No amount of argument could convince them otherwise. Fortunately, our design included a section of roof that could be removed to provide better ventilation in hot weather and this proved useful for pig house clean out as well. Shortly after once such clean out, however, came rain and high winds and the removable roof section removed itself into the next field.

From then until now this splendid structure has required a series of rearguard actions, mostly in response to renovations undertaken by the tenants. This year's crew have been having a delightful time pointing out structural flaws. They've had most of the floorboards up and, in the hot weather a while back, they took off the whole front.

Maybe reinforced concrete is the ticket. We could always put a ring in the roof and when we wanted to move it bring in one of those big construction cranes.

"Is it time yet?" Every year we raised pigs there would come a time when the family members who were looking after their feeding would return from the pig yard with a good deal of whatever was being served distributed randomly about their persons and I would prepare for the inevitable question; "Isn't it about time to ship those pigs?" The answer, alas, was usually "No." I figured the question meant the pigs had reached about 150 pounds. They needed to put on another 50 pounds before the much looked for day arrived. However cute and funny young pigs might be, personality declines rapidly once they reach about 150 pounds. By the time they have reached 200 pounds everybody is happy to see them go.

The pigs are no longer charming. For one thing, they know which bucket has the milk in it and they know all about diversionary tactics. A quick feint with the slops pail used to be enough to send them scurrying to where they thought the milk would land, leaving us enough time to pour the bucket in the other end of the trough. It ain't that way any more.

For one thing, they are now so big they leave very little open space once they are in position at the trough, and they are in position at the trough by the time we are half way to the pigpen from the back door.

For another thing, food is no longer a matter of "Oh, wow! What do you suppose we're going to have this time?" Food has become Big Business, and they are in there for the last round of the big corporate takeover. Toss in the pig chop and they snuffle around in it a bit, raising a small sacrificial cloud of ground barley, but their little piggy eyes are on the slops pail and they are ready for it.

When we moved the electric fence to give them more scope to root out couch grass and other noxious weeds in that part of the garden, they were not interested in crossing the line where the fence had been. In fact, they spent several days in their house. We think they suspected that the fence had been camouflaged and was lurking, waiting to jump out and bite their poor noses, as it had done so many times before. It was at this difficult time in their lives that they moved their toilet indoors, necessitating a cleanup that we would really rather not discuss.

It was, of course, food that finally got them out and about again. Morning and night, we would move the trough just a little bit closer to and finally beyond where the fence had been, and they would groan and moan, their tails would droop, and their eyes would water with trying to see if the fence was still there. But if electrification was a worry with them, the prospect of missing a meal was a positive spectre. So, legs braced, they would follow the trough where it led.

How civilized the supper hour! Neither of them was about to risk electrocution and one could stroll over to the trough with the slops, secure in the knowledge that electrical anguish would hang on for a few minutes before it would be replaced with starvation anguish. Somebody said civilization is only skin deep. That optimistic view of things clashes with porcine psychology. While the trough was moving along, we could walk freely in the new part of the yard and carrying a bucket from the feed barrels to the trough was the work of a moment.

Then came the day when they found out that the fence had departed and they shelved electrical anguish, for the time being at least. Then it was we discovered they had taken up drooling. Since pigs want to be as near the source of food as they can, it was impossible to get out of their yard without being liberally be-slobbered.

Laundry began to pile up at an alarming rate. Our whole approach toward feeding changed. Alice came in one evening and announced that she no longer liked feeding the pigs and when were they going to be shipped? The question arose for the first time this year. It will not be the last time, assuredly. Unfortunately, although they are growing apace they have not yet reached the point where they can cease and desist, travelling off as so many before them have done, in a happy haze of pig claret. For the nonce, the trough has been moved as close to the edge of the yard as is safe.

There was the year we thought the pigs of summer had all developed a simultaneous hiccough. We had come to the point of putting the trough just over the fence from the feed barrels, and, while they were certainly ravenous, every time they would start in on the food they would also begin to do a little dance: chomp, squeal, pull the snout out of the trough, chomp, squeal, etc. It was several feeding times before we twigged that they had shoved the metal trough up against the electric wire. As far as we could tell, it didn't interfere with their digestion. This lot is getting to the point where they wouldn't care either.

We had come from the city in part to be able to have a direct role in the managing of our own food supply. We were not planning to make money by farming. We had, in fact, looked for a place in the country where we could be self sufficient in a small way, where the whole family could have a role to play in this domestic economy and where we would not be taking a working farm out of production.

Our methods of raising pigs, like much else on this place, tended to be experimental in a way that no agricultural scientist would understand. We were concerned with the welfare of all the farm's residents and took pains to be informed in matters of their feed and health.

Improvisation and more-or-less inspired creativity were the hallmarks of our farming methodology. Nowhere was this more evident than in the manner we devised for shipping our pigs in the fall. Basically, we modified some advice given to us after the rather harrowing experience of loading our first pig. Like most of us, pigs are rather conservative creatures and do not take well to sudden changes in circumstances. Pigs are also, like some of us, quite nervous and easily upset. A distressed pig of any size can make a startling amount of high-pitched complaint.

In the case of Grover, our first pig, the distress was harder to take than the noise. After finally getting him loaded into a neighbour's truck, we decided we were not going to put another pig, or any of the rest of us, through that kind of distress again. A neighbour suggested a six-pack of beer as a method of reducing stress for the loading party, but that didn't do anything for the pig. We noted the advice but shelved it. There had to be a better way.

The next year an elderly neighbour came to help with the loading of the three pigs. Don Parlee never seemed to be in a hurry but the amount of work he could get done was staggering. I knew this well, having offered to give him a hand with some woods work shortly after we arrived. I don't think he even took an extra breath, but by noon I was just about played out and all I had done was help him with a few of the lighter tasks. In the matter of loading the pigs, as far as I could tell, (he had sent me off to get a piece of rope, "in case we need it") he simply scattered some grain on the bed of the truck and the pigs had walked up and onto the truck without a single backward glance.

That episode taught us a lesson that has come in handy on many subsequent occasions, with a variety of large animals that were, for some reason, somewhere they shouldn't be. A feed bucket up front was likely to be a far more effective means of guidance than any amount of rope or urging from behind. Armies are not alone in travelling on their stomachs.

While we were impressed by Don's calm handling of the loading, we also knew that we couldn't hope to duplicate a lifetime's experience at the snap of any number of fingers. The next year we had two pigs and as shipping time came closer anxieties rose correspondingly. The answer came from a surprising quarter.

For many years I had enjoyed winemaking as a hobby and had had only a few outright failures. That year I had started a batch of wine from a kit with a "best before" date long past. When it came time to bottle it, it turned out to have an off-flavour. I didn't want to dump four gallons of wine, so it sat in a corner of the basement, undrinkable but equally undumpable.

When the day came to ship the pigs, three things came together in my mind: the suggestion about the sixpack of beer, the question I had asked in all innocence as to whether the beer was for us or for the pigs, and the thought that pigs are enthusiastic about most things edible or drinkable. Most animals are strictly teetotallers, but pigs are not. I knew because I had noted their enthusiasm on the not so rare occasion when I had fed them some discarded fruit pulp that had been used as the base of a new batch of wine. And then I thought of the four gallons of off-flavoured red wine in the basement and a light flashed on in the darkness. Not wasting a moment, I poured off some of the wine into a bucket, filled the bucket with water and advanced on the pig trough.

It worked like a charm. In fact, I was back in the house so soon my wife asked me when I was planning to load the pigs. "They're loaded," I said. And I meant it.

And so, the tradition of a bucket of what we were pleased to call "pig claret" at shipping time was inaugurated. It served both our pigs and us well, year after year except for the time the truck was late…

Chapter 9:
A Bearable Glory

I believe a leaf is no less than the journeywork of the stars.

Walt Whitman
from *Leaves of Grass*

The fuzziness of a busy life is all around us these days. We're told to "stop and smell the roses" or to "be in the moment," but we are conditioned to live for the larger events in life, like weekends, births, or vacations. It's hard to grasp the idea of moving more slowly through life, of respecting the instances of what can only be described as magic in plain sight. From the frost of a winter morning—intricate, pure, and delicate—to the silence of a wide open sky above us, these moments add value to our existence. Just like the sight of a individual four-leafed clover in a field of clover, these small moments in life and nature uplift our spirits and show us the value of the under considered details around us.

> Alice noticed a curiosity as we got up to go inside last evening after a pleasant bask in the sun on the side porch. At first, I didn't see what was so startling. But there it was, a young petunia growing up in a pot of geraniums, not only growing but also blooming. The big planter of petunias right beside it had already given up the ghost. I must say, this young petunia was a cheering sight, making a kind of defiant gesture in the face of nights that get steadily colder and days that get steadily shorter.
>
> Along the driveway, in the deep ditch we had dug last spring, the wild plants are gradually coming back despite the cooling weather. I had occasion to admire them this morning as I took a letter down to the mailbox. What astounded me was the number of different flowers in

that short stretch of what is basically barren subsoil. There were evening primroses (*Oenothera biennis*) and purple-stemmed asters (*Aster puniceus*). There was the fragrant lance-leaved goldenrod (*Solidago graminifolia*) which does not cause hay fever, the so-called common fleabane (*Erigeron philadelphicus*), and tansy ragwort (*Senecio jacobaea*), not to be confused with ragweed, the real cause of hay fever, and even two tiny ground-ivy (*Glechoma hederacea*) plants, sometimes called Creeping Charlie or gill-over-the-ground, one with whitish blossoms and one with deep blue flowers.

The first flowers I saw, however, were the evening primroses with their cheerful yellow four-petal flowers. At least, I've always called them evening primroses partly because that's what my wife tells me they are. In fact, as I found out when I started poking around in the reference books, they really are *evening* primroses; they open in the afternoon and wilt by the afternoon of the next day.

These cheerful flowers belong to the *Onagraceae* family, from the Latin *onager*, a wild ass. The handbooks on wild plants don't say whether the wild ass was fond of these plants as a food source or whether something about the plant made somebody think of a wild ass.

More interesting than wild ass is a connection closer to home. Within the family, its genus is *Oenothera*, which, my Latin dictionary tells me, means "a plant, the juice of which, drunk in wine, produces sleep." And to think, growing right on the driveway. Amazing!

What really got me thinking were the blue flowers. "Michaelmas daisies," I said to myself and then a voice inside my head said, "They're not daisies, they're asters." And I had to admit that, yes, they were asters, but a creeping doubt had me heading back to the house to consult the books. Half an hour later I had run through every wildflower guide and herbal we had and had failed to turn up a reference to Michaelmas daisies. I finally found them in a Stokes Seeds catalogue under the heading "ASTERS (Michaelmas Daisies)."

Working back from Stokes (in looking for the solution to a problem, it always helps if you know the answer), I found our plant, *Aster puniceus*, by its purple stem. These \ starry flowers (the Greek *Aster* means star) connect us with ancient history through their purple stems. *Puniceus* means purple-coloured but it also means Punic, Carthaginian, recalling the great city of North Africa, rival to Rome centuries before the Christian era, from which a dye this colour came.

Finally, though, it was the tiny mounds of ground ivy that I led Alice to when she came back from town. Gill-over-the-ground I had always regarded as a weed—indeed, a pest—but there was no denying the beauty of the tiny flowers with their upper and lower lips, delicate lines of colour, bright yellow throats, and the tidy ivy-like leaves circling the stems. I still don't want it in the garden, but anything that beautiful growing in the most miserable soil can't be all bad. In fact, its popular name, gill, comes from a French word meaning to ferment. Apparently, its leaves were once used to help ferment, or flavour, beer.

How many wonders surround us that we scarcely notice, beautiful in themselves and often, through their names, common or learned, connecting us with those who have lived before us even in distant times and distant lands!

Usually a driveway is, well, just a driveway. We zoom up and down it. Looming traffic on the road is more a concern than what vegetation is coming up in the ditch. Although, I must admit it has been a relief the last little while to see the bare earth begin to sport a little green and the ditch looking a little less like a trial excavation for a reproduction of the Grand Canyon. Previously, if pressed, I could only have said there were some yellow flowers and some blue ones growing there and that would have been that. Paying closer attention and a little research reveals wonders, even in a driveway ditch.

Although it seemed for some time this year that fall wasn't happening here, the colour now seems to have come at once. I had promised my cousin and his wife from Pennsylvania that Canadian Thanksgiving was the high season for colour, and I feared this fall would prove me wrong. But by the time our guests arrived there was nothing to apologize for.

This time of year, I always wish I were more observant. There is so much to see, so much to treasure in what can be seen, so much meaning that slips past my awareness. "Today, if ye will hear his voice, harden not your hearts," the Psalmist says to ancient Israel, and to me, a writer whose ears too often are not filled with hearing or his eyes with seeing.

How do we read the signs that are scattered around us in such profusion? These signs speak of a greater reality that glimmers through the plenty of this and that, a plenty that often seems to clutter up our lives and is kicked away or raked up and bagged for the trash like so many dead leaves.

"I must walk with more free senses," Henry David Thoreau wrote in his Journal on August 24th, a hundred and fifty years ago. "It is as bad to study stars and clouds as flowers and stones. I must let my senses wander as my thoughts, my eyes see without looking." His entry ends with a memo to himself: "Be not preoccupied with looking. Go not to the object, let it come to you."

The greatest poet in the English language in our century, T.S. Eliot, says much the same thing in "Ash Wednesday," published three-quarters of a century later.

"Teach us to care and not to care / Teach us to sit still."

But how hard it is not to be "preoccupied with looking." How hard it is for us not to always intrude ourselves and our concerns and thoughts on the amazing things that surround us. How hard it is for us, ever, to "sit still!"

The big maple tree up behind the house brought me to a standstill the other day. All the leaves on the outside of the tree were an exquisite shade of red-gold. That tree always has something a little different up its sleeve from its neighbours. I might not have noted the colour and tipped my hat to another splendid performance, had not the tree "come to me" one morning in the sunlight.

This tree does not wear all its leaves on its sleeve, so to speak. A lot of leaves seem to live quite happily back in the shadowy recesses closer to the trunk. I'd never really thought about where trees put their leaves or why the shade under that particular tree seems especially dense and pleasant on a hot summer day, until I spotted the green shading inside the red-gold fireworks.

I looked once, then twice. Then I stopped entirely, the milk bucket I was holding and the eggs I was cradling in my sweater forgotten for the moment.

I had been admiring that tree for a number of days. It's a great tree, solitary, standing at the top of the rise along the fence line between the garden and the back pasture, with no competition. Every year it puts on a show that is, as my mother was fond of saying, "a sight for sore eyes." Just the spectacle of all that red-gold against a blue sky is memorable.

But the other day it was the green that stopped me. There, just visible within the golden blaze, were leaves still green with the colour of summer. They were moving with the breeze that set all the tree's branches to dancing. Red-gold is a lovely colour all by itself, but if there is one combination of colours that beats all others, I'd say our maple tree had hit it.

That blaze of glory by itself, splendid as it is, is nevertheless a reminder that as the path of one's life grows ever longer in the past it becomes ever shorter in the future, and that all things, including the leaf and the watcher of the leaf, have an end. "In the midst of life we are in death," the Burial Office reminds us. And yet, within that end there is a green life that knows no end. Perhaps, from where we stand we can but catch the occasional glimpse of it, hidden, perhaps, within the blaze of a maple tree.

It is enough, if only we have eyes to see.

There is something rather final about poplar leaves this time of year. The maples turn brilliant hues of yellow and red, and when the leaves fall the ground is carpeted with colour. When the sun is bright in a blue sky and the maple leaves are lying under the trees, the tree itself and the very air around it seem radiant. The poplars, on the other hand, usually have a brief few days when their leaves turn a clear yellow. This year, however, the two sharp frosts two weeks ago short-circuited all that, and the leaves went from dull green to chocolate brown almost overnight.

Until last night, the poplar leaves hung on the trees, making a leathery rattling sound when the wind stirred them, a sound very different from their lovely whispering in a summer breeze. Now, the ground is littered with their dull brown relics and the yard becomes their potter's field. But even their otherwise unremarkable corpses held a fleeting beauty. As I walked to the barn, I noticed nestled in each popular leaf was a bit of rainwater from the night before. The sun was reincarnated in the raindrops, so that each leaf seemed to hold a diamond that flashed and glittered and promised a life beyond this life.

By the time I go to the barn these evenings, the sun is long gone and the stars are out. I look above me for familiar sights and am aware of what I don't see. Bright Arcturus, that familiar sight above the western horizon in the summer is lost now in the after-glow of sunset. By the time the western sky is dark, the Big Dipper is resting on the northwest horizon of the hill behind us.

Stars shine in the night sky and the poplar leaves wink tiny stars on the ground in the sunshine. And between heaven and earth we have the glory of the maples. What more could a person want of the Creation?

To me the meanest flower that blows can give
Thoughts that do often lie too deep for tears.

William Wordsworth
from "Ode on Intimations of Immortality"

When I was an undergraduate and fascinated by Wordsworth, I thought those two lines very fine. Now, some 40 years later, I think I know what Wordsworth was talking about.

The morning after the ice storm last week the sun came up on a wonderland. There had been enough freezing rain on Tuesday to apply a glaze to trees and bushes but not so much as to cause limbs and branches to snap under the weight. Sometime in the night the temperature had fallen and covered the granular snow on the ground with a fine layer of new powder-like snow. Walking to the barn was like walking through diamond dust under sterling silver trees. A thousand suns flashed from the ground with every step I took. The big rose bush in the dooryard, with its red hips and arching branches, looked like a perfect replica of itself cast in precious metals by an incredibly patient craftsman.

Later in the morning, when I had occasion to walk across the barn pasture, my eye was caught by a small, pale tuft of dried grass next to the wheel of the old dump rake. The sun had not yet reached that part of the pasture. Nothing shouted out for attention in the shadow. Yet my eye stopped on that tuft of fine grass. It was not so much embalmed in the ice as crowned with the most delicate filigree of glass. Beyond all the glories of the morning, it was that insignificant tussock that brought me to a stop. It made me stoop down to see it better, made me think of angelic voices lifted up in praise of One who, out of the intensity of Tuesday's storm, could yet lean down with infinite tenderness and bestow upon a tuft of pasture grass a bearable glory.

The next evening, a friend and I drove into Saint John to hear Maureen Forrester, sponsored by Opera New Brunswick, sing at the Imperial Theatre. The human voice, that tiny set of vibrations in the air, the production of a few bits of muscle working on a tiny measure of breath, seems a puny thing with which to confront the world. And yet, perhaps it's precisely because the human voice is such a puny thing that it sometimes rises to a magnificence that awakens thoughts, which "lie too deep for tears."

It was so that Wednesday night. Alone on stage, except for her accompanist David Warrack at the piano, facing the spaciousness of the theatre, Maureen Forrester stood and sang. The first half of the program included songs by names familiar enough in the realms of classical music, names like Gustav Mahler and Franz Schubert. But she also sang a traditional Berceuse Creole and a Negro spiritual, "Sister Mary," and three Métis folk songs, arranged by Canada's Malcolm Forsyth.

A few years ago, the buzzword in musical circles was "crossover." All kinds of classically trained musicians were suddenly doing jazz or pop, or even rock. A lot of what was produced sounded exactly like classical artists doing jazz or pop or rock.

Maureen Forrester wasn't getting on the crossover bandwagon. She wasn't trying to sound as though she were black when she sang "Sister Mary." Each piece she sang was approached with a humility that was quite wonderful to observe. The lady singing has thirty honorary doctorates from Canadian universities, she has been chairman of the Canada Council, she won the Governor General's Performing Arts Award last year and she is a Companion of the Order of Canada. None of that was allowed to rest heavy on the music. Each piece, from Mahler to Métis, it seemed to me, gave her as much enjoyment as it gave her audience.

The second half of the program was a set of perky, rather tongue-in-cheek explorations of the ups ("From the Cradle to Today") and downs ("Another Night in Another Room") of a performing career composed for her in a variety of musical styles by David Warrack. I had heard about these songs from a daughter who had seen her perform them in Ottawa, and I wasn't sure I was going to like them much. But she brought the same delight to them, as well as a wonderful ability to poke fun at herself. Who wouldn't be charmed?

A tuft of dead grass can have its glory. Even the tiny human voice in an artist like Maureen Forrester can suddenly reveal something so simple and yet so deeply true that it moves us—moves us even beyond tears.

I think that's what Wordsworth was getting at.

And so, at last, the huckstering and silliness is almost over for this year. The great hootchie-kootchie dance of mass merchandising has bopped and bumped and ground its way to its terminal twitches. The last cash register will soon ring up its last sale. Silent too will be the super sweet recordings that tell us to listen because the herald angels have something important to say, only to be interrupted with the more relevant news of a five-minute sale in ladies' lingerie.

However, an un-advertised, un-merchandised, insignificant birth that took place some two thousand years ago on a dark night in a stable in a hick town in a backwater of the greatest empire of all time, still has the ability to cause a hush to fall across the world.

I used to wonder why it was that something, which was to be so important, should start out in a small town that was not much more than the equivalent of a restaurant and a couple of gas stations. There was no Chamber of Commerce. No one from Triple-A or the Michelin Guide had ever been there. No bright lights. Local travelling theatre troupes passed it by. It was, in short, "the sticks."

In the course of more than half a century of wandering I have seen Christmas come and go in the city and on the outskirts of the city. I have seen it in fairly small towns and right out in the country. There were no clear winners or losers among those various places, although there were places I liked better than others. I can't even say that the people were different.

There are good people and not-so-good people, and some stinkers, everywhere. You find what you are looking for, in a way. If you think people in the city are unfriendly you will probably find them that way. If you think people in the country are set in their ways, well, you will probably wind up remembering the things that prove you right.

The first Christmas I remember with certainty was before I started school, when my family was living out in the country in a "house by the side of the road." I don't know about being "a friend to man," but I do remember my mother feeding the occasional tramp in those Depression days, and I remember my father once showing me the marks on a telephone pole down the road a piece, the marks that meant, in tramp code, the next house was one where a hand-out might be hoped for. The dirty, ragged men were scary to me then, and I used to keep out of their way.

Mother and father are both dead now, and, not having brother or sister, I have no one to ask about those days. My father's work kept him away from home, often for weeks at a time. There was no one there but my mother and me. There probably weren't a lot of tramps. We weren't running a soup kitchen, only giving a bit of food to the hungry. But the fact that I remember them at all suggests to me that there were more than one or two. I would like to ask Mother what her feelings were. Certainly, she never gave me any sense of being nervous or apprehensive about the strangers at the gate.

When I started school, we moved from that house into town, and from there, in a couple of years, to another town, and then, a year or so later, to a suburb of a big city; most of my Christmases from then until a few years ago were spent in an urban environment.

The Depression—and the tramps—vanished in the darkness of Pearl Harbour and the Second World War. With the end of the war came a new world and new ways. Neither the Depression nor the tramps were to return. There seemed to be no problem, no hunger, no need that couldn't be conquered by the application of science and technology.

Time passes, as the song says. Many Christmases have come and gone. Problems that seemed to be on the way to being gone for good don't seem that easy to eliminate now. The world looks very much like a replay of the late Roman Empire as it was two thousand years ago when Bethlehem was "the sticks."

In my own wanderings it has come to me that there was good reason why a little place like Bethlehem was picked for the Big Event. I think of the tramps that used to come to our kitchen door out there in the country and I think of the tattered and tired couple that was sent off to sleep in the stable. I'll bet they didn't look like the bright and shiny pair that appear on Christmas cards. And, I'll bet they might have looked a little scary to a youngster who watched them go by, sheltered by the safety of his own comfortable home.

But they weren't headed for the bright lights; they weren't doing one-night stands in the better hotels. They were there because most people aren't born on Broadway, however important and indispensable Broadway may think itself to be.

In the hush that falls on Christmas Eve, "I wonder as I wander" and think it's still possible to hear the cry of the child who was born for all people, however poor, however weak, however unimportant, "poor ornery people like you… and like I."

Merry Christmas!

A friend, looking over a series of these columns once said to me, "You often write about the weather." "Oh no," I thought. "They're on to me"

I suppose my fascination with the weather is the result of years and years of living in what are called residential areas; places where it is hardly possible to know what the world is doing with any finer gauge than "good weather" and "bad weather." Bad weather was subdivided into rainy weather and winter storms. I always rooted for the bad weather; it was so much more interesting than an endless succession of blue skies and light breezes. But I must admit that in the city bad weather was likely to be just a nuisance rather than anything else.

The other morning the outside thermometer read minus five F. The temperature the night before had been plus six F. Somehow minus five felt a lot colder than even lower temperatures last month. Later, when the sun rose, our eyes were delighted with hoar frost sparkling from every bush and tree. Even more magically, an hour later, a mist, under the urgent summons of a white sun, came rising up from the valley in front of us.

Looking down the fields and towards the woods beyond, we saw everything as if it was just emerging from the mists of the first morning, the day the world began. The woods beyond our lower fields were a series of faint suggestions with here or there a larger tree just coming into being—or so it seemed. A change in the weather was surely coming, we said, and how right we were.

Our farm is located in the fold of the hill behind us. This location places us in a middle state where we look out over a wide valley and can watch the weather as it develops. Were we to live in the valley, and be covered by morning fog our horizon would be limited until it burned off. But we would know the day was likely to be fair. Were we to live on the top of the mountain and be covered by morning fog, we would know that the day was likely to bring rain. We might not see much more of the day than one can see from inside a cloud.

Here on our farm, however, the sun beats in our front windows as we look out over the valley filled from one side to the other with a white river of fog; above the fog there is the most glorious freshness everywhere. When the day bodes rain, we can look from the kitchen windows and see the clouds hanging on the hill above us as if caught in the trees. From here, we can see the weather as it unfolds through the day and judge the severity of the storm by how far we can see across the valley.

The earliest speakers of the language we call English knew the ancestor of our word "earth," but when they were thinking of "the dwelling-place of men and animals" they used the word "middan-yeard," which translates roughly as the "middle yard," or, more poetically as "middle earth." For them, there were three realms to the created order. There was the realm of the heavens above us, the realm of the nether regions below us. Earth was the middle ground in more ways than one.

We have lost our place in the cosmos in this modern world, and not gained a great deal in return, at least with regard to our life as human beings. The three-storey universe gave us the central place by right, though not the place of honour. It also "saved the appearances," that is, it accounted for the appearance of things as we see them—something modern science fails to do.

Here on this farm, living between the hill behind us and the valley before us, we too live in a three-storey world. But we also hold a sense of this small world being caught up in a great world that is both beyond us, and with us, represented by the great dome of the heavens arching overhead.

This morning, as I looked out the upstairs window at flakes of sunlight reflected in the quick water running down the driveway where two days ago there had been only the dull gleam of ice, it was hard not to feel the presence of an unexpected blessing falling from the heavens above. How can one not be fascinated by this thing we dismiss so easily, the weather?

"Until I looked at Anna Botsford Comstock's book,
mine was also an 'unrewarded eye.'"

I had never thought, until this spring, how some of the wildflowers of the season—coltsfoot, dogtooth violet, and dandelion, to name three common ones—seem to echo the return of the sun as the days lengthen. Even as the sun's rays gather strength and the trees and grass, dormant since last fall, begin to push out cautious leaves to test the weather, these wildflowers spangle the landscape with bright, sunny spots of yellow.

Especially now, the dandelions, on which we wage war when they take up residence in the gardens, have freckled fields and lawns with myriads of tiny suns. Like its relative the giant sunflower, the dandelion opens its golden blooms when the sun is shining and closes them again when the evening falls or rain threatens.

Anna Botsford Comstock, in her marvellous *Handbook of Nature Study*, now long out of print, blends poetry and prose as she introduces children to the natural world around them. At the beginning of the section on the dandelion she quotes James Russell Lowell's description of this "dear common flower."

> *'Tis the spring's largess, which she scatters now*
> *To rich and poor alike, with lavish hand,*
> *Though most hearts never understand*
> *To take it at God's value, but pass by*
> *The offered wealth with unrewarded eye.*
>
> from "To the Dandelion"

Until I looked at Anna Botsford Comstock's book, mine was also an "unrewarded eye." I had not realized how much there was to see in a mere weed. I had not looked closely at the flower of the dandelion. I had never seen that each yellow ray ends in five petals so tiny they seem more like the teeth of a microscopic saw. Nor had I stopped to consider why is it that the silver-grey globe of seeds, each with its balloon of fuzzy threads, stays intact for a while after its appearance. The head to which the seeds are attached is at first concave and then becomes convex when it opens, liberating the seeds.

In her *Modern Herbal* (another treasure house of lore about plants many have found useful down the years), Mrs. M. Grieve tells me that each leaf in the rosette of dandelion leaves below the flower stems is grooved so that any water falling on the leaves is immediately conducted to the centre of the rosette and so the root is always kept well-watered.

Most people know that the dandelion's common name comes from France, which shows how widespread this plant is. In fact, it grows everywhere in the temperate zone of the Northern Hemisphere. I knew the French name, *dent de lion*, meant lion's tooth, but always thought vaguely that the reference was to the little petals of the flower and wondered why the French thought lions had yellow teeth. But, as Prof. Comstock reminds me, it is the particular way the leaves are shaped, with their jagged appearance that reminds one of teeth.

Even the most humble of names, and often those names especially, carry a meaning that leads us in the direction of what was, until quite recently, the profound insights of humble people about the interconnectedness of things. Before the advent of machines people had to observe their surroundings minutely and learn to work with what was given. No talk then in relation to the world around them of a "war on weeds" and none of the vocabulary of military might that comes so easily to us today was applied against the natural world.

Why then were the jagged leaves of the dandelion thought to represent the teeth of the lion, a decidedly exotic beast in that part of the world in which dandelions flourish? Why not wolf's teeth or cat's teeth or something familiar? The answer probably lies deep in the folk perception that the world and all the richness of the created order are not so many "things" external to us to be, at best, noted down, put on a list, and cast aside. All Creation from the serene, unchanging stars overhead to the chaotic waters of the oceans meant something beyond their appearance; every feature of Creation was a sign pointing to a deeper meaning.

A sign on one level of being echoed another sign at another level of being, thus signalling the Creator's hidden presence, no matter what aspect of the world one was attentive to.

To this way of experiencing the world, to this way of thinking, the golden sun in the heavens, the gold in the earth, the golden lion ("king of beasts" in the animal kingdom), the golden eagle in the air, even the humble golden dandelion at our feet among the plants all spoke of light; the light of day, yes, but also of the "light which lighteth every man which cometh into the world" (John 1:9.)

In the old way of thinking that we now dismiss as pre-scientific, fire and water are not entirely opposites. Along with earth and air, they make up the substance of the visible creation. The ancient Egyptians, for example, thought of the sun, that source of fire, as being kindled each morning from the waters at the edge of the world.

This old way of seeing things, with its apparent simplicity, gave a reasonable and quite workable description of how humans saw the world. What it also did, as we often forget, was to connect everything in creation with a larger world that did not appear directly. In a way, this worldview was just like ours; it appealed to things not seen to explain the things that are seen.

I have never seen an atom or a molecule, yet I can quite happily talk about atoms and molecules. I can even list off at least some of the elements that make up the Periodic Table because scientists who work with these kinds of things assure me this is what lies within the apparently solid form of my gold ring or my steel hammer.

But our forebearers had their own experts who, by dint of a discipline at least as arduous as that of modern scientists, were prepared to speak with authority about the invisible world that informed the whole of the visible world. It wasn't that they didn't know that gold was gold. What they sought was not physical properties in ever increasing minuteness but the spiritual properties of what they knew to be a created order; properties which, rightly understood, would lead them to the Author of that order.

The other day, that old way of seeing things seemed not old at all. It was a day that began in water and ended in fiery thunderbolts.

There was no fog on the mountain that morning betokening a rainy day, and no fog in the valley prophesying a sunny one. Our whole little world was wrapped in fog. As an invisible sun presumably rose in an eastern sky the only effect was to intensify a greyness that was almost palpable.

It was one of those mornings when this solid world we take for granted suddenly dissolves and we grope our way as if transported into a world only just now coming into being, as if we were walking on the waters of the first creation when objects had not yet entirely gained their substance and were still rather tentative. There was not a breath of air. As I walked to the barn our little world was like a beloved face never to be forgotten but whose outlines have grown dim in the mind.

Gradually, the fog thinned and withdrew into higher clouds as the day advanced, but the sky remained largely grey. Some time after the sun had set in a grey sky behind us and dusk was gathering in the valley and on all the hills, we walked up to the garden to move the soaker hose.

"Look at that!" Alice exclaimed, pointing away to the east. I looked, and there rising up in the sky was a huge dome shaped thunderhead, rising so high it was crowned with a skullcap of ice crystals. Black at the bottom, it towered up beyond our evening into a day beyond our day, rose and purple and gold, luminous and majestic. It looked as if all the mist of the morning was gathering in response to the Psalmist's words: "He bowed the heavens also, and came down: and darkness was under his feet. And he rode upon a cherub, and did fly: yea, he did fly upon the wings of the wind."

Darkness and light, water and fire; even as we watched, a bolt of lightning flashed from the very top of this vaporous mountain to the ground. Again and again, bright streaks hurtled down from the summit of the cloud as if hurled by a mighty arm. The piled glory of that cloud seemed right before us, yet it was so far away we never heard the thunder.

A few moments later, we had finished moving the soaker hose to another part of the garden and when we looked again toward the east the cloud was gone. The world was grey again. Night was falling. But what a day it had been! The Preacher was right: "As thou knowest not what is the way of the spirit, nor how the bones do grow in the womb of her that is with child: even so thou knowest not the works of God who maketh all" (Ecclesiastes 11:5).

We had seen some clues though.

Past and future gather to the present along a path or a highway travelled back and forth over time. For the past twelve years or so, I have had occasion to travel along the Trans-Canada Highway and its tributaries between Fredericton to the west, and Sackville to the east.

For some reason I can't explain, it's the houses I have seen along the way that have become landmarks for me and remain in memory. Some of them could be called distinguished, like the house toward Fredericton with barge boarding that looks like wooden icicles. This neat little house was empty for a while and then recovered from potential decay thanks to someone whom I imagine to be a university professor on no more grounds than the grey Volvo that is often parked in the driveway.

Some of the buildings are undistinguished architecturally but memorable in other ways, like the house near Petitcodiac that reminded me of the famous 19th century poem "The House By the Side of the Road," by Sam Foss. It was no more than a little white-painted one-storey affair with a bit of front yard and a bit of fence around the yard. What made it special was that a piece of the old highway still ran between it and the new highway making it truly the house by the side of the road by the side of the road. Alas, progress widened that stretch of the highway and one day, where the little house had stood, there was a weigh scale and big dump trucks rolling through. If I look carefully, I can still locate the spot where it stood and imagine it back again.

At one time, that house had a particular meaning for me because, if I were driving away from home, it was the point at which I felt I was leaving familiar territory. Or, if I was returning, I marked the odometer and knew that in so many more miles I would be home.

I attached stories to a lot of the houses I passed, stories I had time to spin out while driving. Whether the stories had any foundation in fact was quite beside the point. There was a house almost at Riverglade, which for years seemed to me caught out of the present day into a sheltered calm time of its own. Why should a structure or even a particular slant of sunlight suddenly pierce us with nostalgia or a timeless presence? What undiscovered kinship do we have with places we have never known directly but which nevertheless whisper to us of a part of ourselves as yet unrecognized?

This bungalow, neatly painted white and black, tidy sheer curtains at the windows, the neatly painted garage across the dooryard, and the neatly planted vegetable garden on the other side of the house, seemed unchanged from its building in the 1930s. It seemed as if it would be possible to walk into that house and disappear into a time that had never ceased to be. Would the newspaper on the kitchen table always be today's but a today of sixty years ago? I will never know.

One day the house was empty when I drove past, and a few months later there was a big pile of used tires in the drive and a couple of late-model cars that had seen better days. Now the house is just another house on a busy section of a commerce-ridden highway, nothing to look at a second time or give a second thought to.

When we first started travelling these roads there was a house near Fredericton that obviously had a story to tell. Covered with that red asphalt siding known as Insulbrick, it sat in a yard protected from the highway by a thirty-foot-high hedge of Lombardy poplars. Lombardy poplars are rare enough around here, but what caught my imagination was the tidiness of the place although it was obviously empty. Insulbrick was never a siding used on fancy houses, and this two-storey farmhouse was no architectural gem. Plain and practical, it had served its owners well, and then, when they were done with it, it had been left to stand empty. What made it different from other abandoned houses one sees around the country were the tidy ruffled curtains that still hung in every window. Though it was empty, someone had cared for it enough to keep the curtains at the windows and close the doors against vandals.

As the years wore on, the doors were broken down, the curtains were ripped or torn away entirely, and other stories impinged; whoever had remembered and cared for the old house had turned their attention elsewhere. Then one day on the way to Fredericton, I remembered that I hadn't seen it. On the way back I looked more carefully. Fire had done what someone had been unable or unwilling to do. There was nothing left of the old house save a few charred timbers. The poplars, though, are still there, witness to the story.

The bergamot mint, tall enough now to lift its flowers well above the edge of our kitchen porch, gladdens us all summer with scarlet blooms that are loved by hummingbirds and look as though Dr. Seuss designed them.

There is a story to this clump of bergamot. It came to us as a gift from someone we never knew, someone who lived maybe a hundred years ago or more on a farm at the top of Bullmoose Hill a few miles from our small farm.

Real estate development is creeping up the southern edge of Bullmoose Hill where the height and lay of the land open up a long vista down the peaceful valley below. So far, though, the height of land and the long rugged spine of the hill have been little touched by the twentieth century. Alice and I drive up there by times to admire the view out across the valley.

On one of our excursions we noticed a few bright flowers amongst a jumble of weeds in what had obviously once been cleared ground. We stopped to explore and soon found a depression in the weeds that was the trace of a cellar-hole. It was all that was left of what once had been a home. But flowers someone had planted and tended were still blooming around the cellar hole in spite of all the long years of neglect.

We carefully dug up a few survivors and brought them back our farm to see if they might once again be encouraged to flourish. The bergamot that now makes such a splash of colour outside our kitchen was just a few thin stems back then. It is impossible to look at it now and not think of the farm wife who tended it up there on Bullmoose Hill. Perhaps she had it from some friend, who had it from a friend, who…

And now, like a gift from someone we never knew, we will tend it for a while, and enjoy it all the more because it is, like all things beautiful, not our possession but a gift.

There is something special, I think, in waifs and strays like this bergamot. One can always open a seed catalogue and find the same thing after some searching and no doubt get a "new and improved" strain for a price. But we like the old and unimproved varieties, the kind that have survived our long winters and the neglect that ensues when a once busy dooryard falls silent, and the wild, that had been pushed back with great effort, once again moves in to reclaim its own.

How pleasing it is to see the scraggly stragglers dug up and transplanted to a bed where they can survive without having to struggle with the more aggressive weeds for a bit of light and nourishment. Here, they can begin to rise and flourish and, in the case of the bergamot, establish itself not as a single stem but as a clump with a triumphant crown of flowers.

The bergamot was all but buried in the thick grass when we found it, shouldered aside by burdocks and overshadowed by goldenrods, but still hanging on in spite of weeds, an old bedspring, bits of china, and shattered fragments of what had perhaps been a parlour stove. Like the flowers in Gray's "Elegy Written in a Country Churchyard," the plants seemed

> *... born to blush unseen,*
> *And waste their sweetness on the desert air.*

Set about, as it was, by signs of ruin and decay, this waif moved us by virtue of its apparent fragility and by what it said, and still says, about the human spirit. Blooming among the ruins, it spoke eloquently of the permanence of hope, and the persistence of beauty.

Driving down back roads when we first came here, we were struck by the apple trees growing, seemingly in the middle of nowhere. But when we got out and poked around a bit, we were sure to find, somewhere near the apple trees, a lilac bush or two, and, not far from the lilacs, the weedy depression in the ground bordered by a rough rectangle of stones—the trace of the house that had once risen above it.

We also found the site of the first house on this farm, now in the midst of woods and completely overgrown. During a summer afternoon's ramble down by the stream at the very far edge of the property, we were startled to notice an apple tree hanging on in spite of the overarching canopy of taller trees. Then, a moment later, we found a lilac and close to the cellar hole, a rose bush. Why should we have been a surprised?

It's really ugliness that is fleeting, not beauty. Sometimes it seems the whole of modern culture is bent on convincing us of the characteristic and enduring human penchant for creating ugliness. "Nice guys finish last" and "if you want to make an omelette, you have to break some eggs," we are told. Boy, as a society, do we know about breaking eggs! Crush! Smash! Splatter!

But then there is the evidence of those abandoned farmyards with their apple trees, their lilacs, their bergamot beloved of hummingbirds, their Maltese cross, day lilies, roses, and all the rest. Can we really look at the evidence and convince ourselves that every one of those abandoned farms is to be understood as a shrine to failure? Can we really convince ourselves that every one of those places represents the spinning-out of a tale of defeat and the springing-up of ugly weeds like hatred and despair and their triumph over tenderness, hope, and love?

The flowers give a contrary witness. Apple trees may have represented a prudent concern for survival through the long winters, but flowers? Flowers are "good for nothing" in economic terms. And yet, after all of what economics would recognize as evidence of human activity has fallen into ruin, the flowers are still blooming. They continue to testify to someone's hope, and someone's delight in beauty, even when the memory of those who hoped has perished.

The pages of guides to wildflowers, published in almost as wild profusion as the flowers themselves, have a phrase that appears again and again—"escaped from cultivation." That sounds as if cultivation was a species of imprisonment, but that isn't so. Rather, as these remnants of domestic cultivation testify, hope, beauty and, yes, even love itself continue to radiate outward as fragile as the ripples on a pond—and as unstoppable.

Chapter 10: O Ye Stars of Heaven

Enlightenment is like the moon shining in a puddle of water. The water is not broken, nor does the moon get wet.

Dogen
13th century Japanese Buddhist teacher

Eight days after His birth, obedient to the ritual laws of the Jews, the child was circumcised, and given his name: God the Saviour, Jesus. He, who created all the starry heavens and all of Nature, is given a name. He, who created time, enters time.

If we raise our eyes to look at where we are in the widest terms, we can say we are a part of the galaxy we call the Milky Way. This great flattened pinwheel of 100 billion stars, with our own star located out on one of the spiral arms, continues to hurtle through space, covering the distance between here and Montreal every second. That works out to about two-and-a-half million kilometres an hour. At speeds like this, we may well ask where is it exactly we are going. We are clearly not headed for the nearest doughnut shop.

Astronomers have an engaging way of talking about the unimaginable depths of empty, or nearly empty, space. They talk about the "local group," for example, and mean a collection of maybe 30 galaxies of which the Milky Way marks one end. The Great Spiral Nebula in Andromeda is the most spectacular example. This local group spans a distance of about 4 million light years, quite a distance when you consider that light can travel more than 300,000 kilometres in one second and more than a trillion kilometres in an hour.

The question of where we are going gains some cogency when the same searchers of the skies tell us that not only our cosy local group, but everything from the Perseus cluster some 300 million light years in one direction to the Hydra-Centaurus cluster 200 million light years in another is rushing toward an unknown destination.

Our Milky Way, and all the other galaxies—a great silent flight of numberless suns—are rushing through the immensities of empty space like iron filings drawn to some huge but hidden magnet. Viewed against the startlingly changeless backdrop of those same stars, our small speck of Earth moves along its path around the sun year by year, which changes the configuration of the zodiac in which spring occurs slightly more than one sign every two thousand years. Who can say what meaning lies in all of this?

What we do know is that in some way, which cannot be put into words, all this motion, near and far, has something to say to us and about us. If nothing else, it reminds us that what we think of as "our" life and "our" times, extends outward in space and backward in time to unimaginable deeps and that we do not know the meaning of the whole pattern or whether the part is bound to the whole by linked chains of cause and effect.

Chaos theory, that branch of science sometimes called non-linear physics, knows of systems in which chaotic or random events lead to apparently stable conditions, at least for a period of time. Is it possible that the tough yet fragile balance of forces we know as "the earth and all that therein is" is just such a momentary stay against confusion, a delicate balance which could, by our own vaulting ambition, be tipped back into chaos?

It is good to be able to let one's imagination roam the universe, from interstellar space to the garden plot behind the house. Winter gives us time for reflection. I get through the season by reminding myself of how soon the hounds of spring will be on winter's traces (as Swinburne said) and using the cold clear nights to watch the skies.

Some people have all the luck. For example, take the case of Alice and me and our birthdays. This question of her birthday and mine has been a problem of long standing. This year she got to have her birthday on Easter Sunday.

When I was a young sprout, I don't remember birthdays being a problem. As a matter of fact, my birthday had some status in the world and was a subject of comment, since the first day of spring and I came into the world together. (Well, not actually, since the first day of spring has been around a lot longer than I have, as incredible as that may seem to my offspring. But the day on which I first presented myself for the awe and admiration of the world at large happened to be the first day of spring that year.)

My small claim to fame has rested secure for most of my life, since the almanac duly noted the arrival of the vernal equinox each year, and each year it was on my birthday. Unfortunately for me, the vernal equinox has a tendency to run a bit fast. That is to say, Earth in its peripatetic wanderings around the sun doesn't get back to exactly the same spot in its orbit at the same moment each year. Those who know about these things call this untidiness in the motion of Earth's travels around the sun the "precession of the equinoxes."

The ancient Greeks were interested in this apparent movement of the first day of spring. They marked out groups of stars, seen as twelve constellations, through which the sun appeared to move in the course of the year. Keen observers that they were—and they didn't have to contend with neighbours having huge banks of lights fit to turn night into day—they noticed that the sun's apparent motion across the sky gradually slipped backwards through these constellations. They figured out exactly how long it would take the sun, year by year, to proceed all the way around the twelve constellations.

It was a big number back then and it's still quite a considerable length of time, even in these days of inflation and currency devaluation. The Greeks thought it was the length of time it took the world to move through the Golden Age, the Silver Age, the Bronze Age, and the Iron Age—the four ages of the world. At the end of the Iron Age (the age they were in and we are still in) something (I'm not quite sure what) would happen and the whole process would start over with another Golden Age.

Back in their day, the sun at the time of the spring equinox was in the constellation of Aries, the Ram. Astrologers, people who make it their business to cast horoscopes, still speak of the time of the vernal equinox as being in the sign of Aries. Unfortunately, time does not stand still and neither does the sun in its peregrinations around the circle of the twelve constellations. The sun is no longer anywhere near the constellation of the Ram on the first day of spring, but people keep behaving as if it were.

This has always made it hard for me to get too excited about horoscopes and the like. A horoscope that is calculated as if the sun were someplace it hasn't been since 500 B.C. might have a bit of a problem. The big sum of money that the newspaper star-gazer has promised me, not to mention the scads of new and interesting friends, may have been waiting for me in the Post Office in ancient Athens twenty-five hundred years ago.

All this precessing of the equinoxes, however, has had a serious effect on my birthday. The terrible truth is, that in the years since I was born, the sun has failed to make it to the starting gate by a few minutes more each year. The few minutes, uninteresting though they may be when taken one by one, have a way of piling up over time, and they have moved the time of the equinox from the day I was born and stuck it back on the day before. I tell you, the world is falling apart. Now all I can claim, and few seem to be impressed, is that my birthday is the first full day of spring.

What I did not take into account as I grew up was the location of the first day of spring in the year as the Church calendar reckons it. It is only as a grown man that I have become aware of Lent. And there is where the birthday problem with my wife comes in. My birthday is always in the middle of Lent, a time of penitence and fasting. Her birthday is exactly three weeks later than mine, which is either in Easter season, or, just to rub it in, she gets to have her birthday on Easter day itself, when joy and celebration can be unconfined.

Some people have all the luck.

When I go out to the barn in the early evenings now, and look to my left across the valley in the darkening sky, the planet Jupiter is rising in the southeast, just about where the Dog Star, Sirius, had been last winter. If I look to my right, above the hill behind us, at first all I see is the afterglow of the sunset, but with a little searching I will spot the Evening Star, Venus, shining through the afterglow following the sun down into the northwest. Venus eludes me, sometimes, even though I know she is there. I scan the glow of the departed sun, thinking thin clouds are in the way, and then, suddenly, the bright point of light is there, clear as can be, even though I had looked at that spot five times before.

Five bodies that can be seen with the naked eye move through the heavens against the background of the so-called fixed stars. The Greeks called them *Planetes*, "the wandering ones." Although we have forgotten the root meaning of the word, we still call Mercury, Venus, Mars, Jupiter and Saturn "planets." Not all of them are visible at any one time. Because of their wandering, they are sometimes too close to the sun's glare to be seen at all either in the morning sky in advance of the sunrise, or in the evening sky following the sunset. Venus and Jupiter, far brighter than the brightest star, are the only representatives of the five now visible in the evening sky.

In the Middle Ages, the number of the wanderers was thought to be seven, and they were listed in order of their distance from Earth, which was regarded as the centre of the cosmos. Closest to Earth, of course, was that very conspicuous wanderer, the moon. The moon was not only the nearest planet, but it was also the boundary between this earthly realm of change and decay and the eternal and unchanging heavens. We still speak, on occasion, of the "sublunary" world, the world below the moon, when we are thinking of the changes and chances of this mortal life.

Beyond the moon, in order of their increasing distance from Earth, were reckoned Mercury, Venus, then (to our surprise) the sun, then Mars, Jupiter, and Saturn. The presence of the sun here need not surprise us if we consider that this classification was based on movement, and the sun is clearly one of those bodies that wanders through the sky, not only in the course of a day's rising and setting but also in its movement from high up in the sky in the summer to near the horizon in the winter.

In treatises contrasting the modern view of the heavens with the ancient view, much is made of the inability of the old system to account for the actual motions of the planets, insisting instead on perfectly circular motions. Much is made, too, of the supposedly egotistical way in which ancient man assumed his Earth was the centre of everything. But the old system was based on what can be seen by Everyman standing in his own dooryard, or out in the fields guarding the sheep on some Mediterranean hillside. The centrality of Earth is obvious to the observer used to watching sun, moon, planets, and stars rising in the east, circling overhead, and setting in the west.

If we put behind us everything we "know" about the heavens through the organizing lenses of science, and simply go out in the dooryard over many evenings and look up with attention, we may be surprised to find that much that is dismissed as pre-scientific or worse is really only a different way of organizing what we know and makes perfect sense from its own standpoint.

Elusive Venus, to my eyes playing hide-and-seek in the sun's light, suggests the limitations of our powers with respect to the larger world around us. I think I see what is to be seen, and yet I can look at the brightest planet in our sky and not see it. Those who long ago and without any of the immensely complicated equipment of modern astronomy, followed the paths of the wanderers and of the fixed stars, and found in those things patterns of importance for their lives, were not fools. Their questions sought not physical data but spiritual truth, and the answers they found brought heaven and Earth together in a wonderful way.

At about half past eight last night the sky above the hill at the back of the farm had the luminous blue of a Maxfield Parrish painting with "the new moon holding the old moon in its arms" (the faint glow of the whole moon resting in the crescent of the new moon). Venus hung above the moon, nicely spaced on a diagonal to the left, with Jupiter, at an equal distance, further on. If someone were to paint that sky and put those three lights in a line like that, the critical reaction would no doubt be, "Contrived, too artificial." But Nature gets away with this all the time.

Growing up in or near cities I had never understood much about the night sky. City lights make it hard to see the sky. Last summer, friends visited us at the farm and pointed out some of the sky's landmarks—skymarks, really. I have been keeping an eye on some of the goings on above us, ever since. Now I am beginning to see how the sky changes from hour to hour, and season to season, and how the planets dance to a different drummer, wandering along on their own pathways against the background of the fixed stars.

Jupiter has been a presence, at least since the winter, when I finally sorted him out from some fairly bright stellar company over in the southeast. Venus is hard to miss, as bright as she is, and following the sun as closely as she does (when she isn't preceding Jupiter up in the sky in the early morning). Mars was up there too last night but not bright enough to stand out against the afterglow. In the middle of next month, if the sky is clear, we should be able to see all three planets and the moon huddled together in one little corner of the sky, a rare event indeed.

For me, though, the real gift my friend gave me was a chance to search the sky with some attention to detail. At that point I was only interested in figuring out which of the many bright points of light in the southeast sky were bright stars, and which were planets passing through.

Mars wasn't too hard to catch, as I recall, since it moved fairly quickly. The Red Planet moved right along as December lengthened. And then, sometime around January, I saw something I imagine not too many have ever seen; Mars stopped in its tracks. It just stopped!

For a long time Mars seemed to be suspended between Taurus and the Pleiades. Night by night I would look up, on my trip to the barn, and there it would be, as if it had decided to take up permanent residence. And then, even more amazing, it began to move backward, almost but not quite, retracing the path it had followed a month before. Finally, having backtracked for a while, it again reversed its course and when I last saw it this spring, it was moving on, above and beyond the seven sisters (Pleiades) and their friends in that part of the sky.

Even as I watched the S curve of Mars's path, night-by-night, I knew I was watching something that had caused faithful watchers of the sky much thought and even astonishment down through the ages.

Everyone knows that the sun rises in the east and sets in the west (well, almost everyone). Not so many people know that the stars follow the same course, spinning through the heavens in their appointed rounds.

If one watches the movement of the sun and the moon and the stars with an eye open to the wonder of it all, it's easy to see why sensible people long thought of the sky as a series of concentric spheres turning around the smallest sphere of all, Earth. From the moon on down all was subject to change and decay. Beyond the moon there was only the serene and endless singing of sphere turning within sphere: Mercury, Venus, the sun, Jupiter, Saturn, and the greatest sphere of all, the sphere of the fixed stars.

And yet, Mars's little backstep shook the whole crystalline structure. This anomaly, together with other troubling little details, would shatter the glassy dome of heaven itself and hurl the tiniest sphere, our Earth, into empty space, to wander who knows where.

Those whose business it is to watch the sky, no doubt see many more wonderful things than Mars's backstep. For this year, though, I'm content.

Alice and I were talking about paintings again as we drove back from a church service up-country last week. It was a beautiful day of summer, blue sky and great pillars and mounds of puffy clouds that never seemed to get in the way of the sun, except to annotate the contours of the hills on the other side of the river by tracing across them, over and over.

"It's the sort of day that would have had John Constable reaching for the paints," I said.

"Yes," Alice said, "but big landscapes don't seem to be in right now."

I came back to the subject as we turned off the highway toward the ferry and looked at the wide expanse of the St. John River. The fields, wetlands, hedges, and trees were low and peacefully domestic in a great sweep from northeast to southeast. The greens and browns and blues of water and land, with piled clouds of whites and greys like visionary Alps, rose, dissolved, and reassembled behind and above the landscape.

"I don't know," I said, "I think if I were a painter, I'd want to paint that."

I've been watching clouds lately. Partly, I am looking for any faint sign of rain to break the drought that is a seemingly endless eight weeks old around here. But partly I am just watching clouds. Recently, it has been high clouds. One morning, the whole zenith was feathered over with the most luxurious collection of mare's tails I can remember seeing. That same evening, sure enough, the waxing moon was looking as though it was shining through ground glass. In a normal summer those two signs in sequence would surely presage rain in a day or two, but this has not been a normal summer and "all signs fail in a drought." The next morning, though, was grey, and before the day was out, we had a shower or two. Even though the showers did no more than dampen the dust in the garden, at least the signs had been right.

This past week I have been admiring the classic summer cumulus. It was the cumulus clouds that had so drawn my eye that Sunday driving home. This visible delineation of vast currents of warm, moist air soaring sunwards start in the lower sky and rise up and up and up. They rise vertically like the soul in its ascension from the bondage to the ten thousand things Buddha spoke of. "Who has seen the wind? Neither you nor I," Christina Rossetti wrote. But anyone who has watched a fog moving in ghostly mysteriousness across a landscape, or watched a great bank of thunderheads building, can answer the question in the affirmative.

Late last night, after guests had departed, I went to the barn and was just in the process of setting things to rights for the morning when Alice came in.

"You really have to see this," she said without indicating exactly what "this" was.

I followed her out into an evening now almost completely dark. Not even a vestige of the sun's influence remained beyond the mountain behind us. Overhead were the bright stars of the summer triangle, Vega, Deneb and Altair, with the Milky Way sweeping in a grand arc up from the east, over our heads and down again in the western sky beyond the trees at the edge of the paddock, its highest point just slightly to the right of the zenith. There to our right, still fairly low in the southeast, was unblinking Jupiter.

It was a fine summer evening with the clear sky that has been such a feature of our summer this year. The Perseid meteor shower of dust and debris had burned itself out in the upper atmosphere a week or so earlier. I hadn't heard of any comets appearing to rival Hale-Bopp, now disappeared on its unimaginable silent journey beyond the solar system. What was there to see?

And then it happened. Over in the northeast and so low on the horizon as to be hardly noticeable were two or three cumulus clouds. From our perspective they seemed to be ranked one behind the other. What showed us their shape and size was not the blotting out of the stars behind them; it was their sudden illumination from within.

I almost didn't see the heat lightning the first time. I only saw the stars blink, as if a celestial flashbulb had gone off, then all was dark again. I certainly saw it the next time as it lit up the clouds and for a moment made them look like the great clouds of interstellar dust seen through a powerful telescope.

The heat lightning I remember from my childhood in Pennsylvania was more of an intermittent glow on the horizon, disembodied, impersonal. The heat lightning we saw last night was neither. It was all the more impressive for being so near, apparently, and yet so silent. Lighting up the clouds, it was like the aureole around the head of a saint in a medieval picture.

Emily Dickinson confessed she was an "inebriate of air and debauchee of dew." It's also possible, I find, to be drunk on clouds.

"If you want to see Mars, you'd better come quick because clouds are moving in!"

We had guests from the States who, unfortunately, were not close readers of that indispensable source of astronomical knowledge, *The Old Farmer's Almanac*. Nevertheless, we had succeeded in turning the conversation to the current wonder in the night sky—the closest approach of the "angry planet" to Earth in 60,000 years.

I'm not one of those who long for a telescope. There are several reasons for this, the first, and principle, being that whatever I had would not be as big as the Hubble Space telescope. Once the pictures that the Hubble has taken are published, anything less seems dust and ashes. Heck, even the 200-inch Mount Palomar telescope, the wonder of my youth, is just another telescope these days. Try putting that in your backyard.

I've even given up buying copies of Sky News; too many articles about the latest expensive gadgets for your personal observatory. And anyway, the folklore of the sky is a lot more fun than going on about light-years and parsecs ("a unit of measure for interstellar space equal to a distance having a parallax of one second as measured from diametrically opposite points on Earth's orbit or to 3.26 light-years"). I have enough trouble establishing diametrically opposite points on the edges of a one-by-six piece of lumber.

The Greeks called the Red Planet, Ares. They thought the divine figure represented by the planet was the son of Zeus and his consort Hera. The other heavenly denizens, according to the great epic poet Homer in his *Iliad*, disliked the murderous, angry, and bloodstained Ares. Unlike the later Romans, the Greeks were not fond of Ares.

Mars, of course, is the name we get for this planet from the Romans. According to legend, the god Mars fathered a pair of twins, Romulus and Remus. Their mother was Rhea Silvia, daughter of Numitor, king of Alba Longa. His younger brother, Amulius, forced Rhea to take a vow of chastity and deposed Numitor. Subsequently, when she bore the twins, Amulius ordered the infants drowned in the river Tiber. However, the trough in which they were placed floated down the Tiber and came to rest at the future site of Rome. There, a woodpecker and a female wolf—animals sacred to Mars— fed and suckled the infants until they were found by Faustulus, a herdsman. The twins, who were brought up by Faustulus and his wife, eventually killed Amulius and restored Numitor to the throne. They later founded Rome on the site where they had been saved.

In Roman thought, Mars was second in importance only to Jupiter. Mars was variously interpreted as a god of agriculture, spring, and war. The symbol still used to represent Mars—a circle with an arrow projecting from it—is a reduced form of the representation of a shield and a spear. We still have a weekly commemoration of Mars in our word Tuesday (compare French Mardi, Mars's day), which is derived from Tiu, the Germanic god equivalent to Mars.

This summer has not been a good time for paying attention to the sky. Even when the sky has been clear in the daytime it has tended to cloud up after sundown. And so, as August began, I was fretting a bit because, according to *The Old Farmer's Almanac*, Mars was getting closer to Earth at a rate of some millions of miles every day, and I couldn't even see the moon. Thursday of last week was the point of maximum approach, when Mars was as close as it can be and closer than it has been since a long time before human beings were paying attention.

So, the other night, when I rushed outside to see if I could spot the planet rising across the valley, I had only seen it once about ten days before. After peering into the deepening dusk, I thought I caught a glimpse of it, somewhat east of south, a bright orange-yellowish ball quite close to the horizon and apparently about to disappear into a cloud bank above it. After I had gathered everybody up and dragged them down to the yard where we could all see Mars, it was Alice who gently pointed out that what we were looking at was a dusk-to-dawn light across the valley.

I have seen Mars (really!) several times since then. Even if you missed it last week, it will still be rather bright for the next few days. The next chance to see it so close will be in 2287. I don't know about you, but I don't expect to wait around.

Alice and I are probably the last people in the world to see the new wonder in the skies, the comet with a name that sounds like a greeting studded with exclamation points; "Hale! Bopp!" I have to admit that one reason why we hadn't seen it earlier was a devotion I have long had to sound sleep in the early hours of the morning. All the information we had suggested that the best time to view Hale-Bopp was in the morning about an hour before the beginning of dawn's early light. Well, frankly (this is no triumphalist statement), I don't do sunrises, let alone the hour before dawn.

It has always seemed to me that one the of merciful gifts of a kind Creator was to put a fine display of dramatic effects in the sky at sundown, thus sparing us non-morning persons the guilt attendant on missing the sunrise.

This present comet and the one last year with the Japanese name (Hyakutake) seemed to be some sort of celestial apology for the great fizzle of Halley's Comet, the most spectacular of all the periodic comets, on its last fly-by in 1986. On the occasion of a total eclipse of the sun when I was old enough to notice such things, I remember elderly relatives talking about the splendid apparition Halley's made in 1910 and how fortunate I would be because I would see it when it returned in 1986.

Well, I didn't see it. I did look, a couple of times, but even professional comet watchers agreed it was nothing to write home about. The comet that had first been noticed by humankind in 466 BC had gone by, and I figured the chances were rather slim that I would be taking an interest in comets, periodic or otherwise, in 2062 when it was due back again.

Twenty-nine times Halley's Comet had passed by since 466 and made enough of an impression to get into the pages of history. Nineteen sixty-eight was one of the few times it hadn't been enough of a show to bring even the observant out on their front lawns to gawk at it.

A typical headline about the present comet says something rather smug about how comets used to be thought warnings of divine anger, but not anymore. With our greater knowledge of what is really going on, comets no longer terrify us; I wonder how much we really know?

Granted, we can now determine the orbit of a comet down to any number of decimal places. We can tell whether its orbit is elliptic, parabolic or hyperbolic. We can even somehow tell how big the thing is. A really huge comet in 1811 had a tail that stretched 130 million miles, and the Great Comet of 1843 had a tail 200 million miles long. We can predict when some comets, like Halley's, will return. There are 50 or so who come back more than once a century.

On the other hand, some comets just boggle the mind with the extent of their travels. The comet of 1811 comes back about every 3,000 years and a comet seen in 1864 is thought to take more than two million years to make the round trip. That orbit would take it more than half a light-year out into interstellar space before making the turn and starting back again. That's quite a distance!

There is something awesome in the thought of the black unknowable emptiness far, far beyond the boundaries of the solar system. This emptiness is filled with the cobweb tracery of lumps of dirty ice each moving silently along its own path. At some point, they slow and then turn and start back to a rendezvous with small stars that to us are so remote as to be indistinguishable from all the other pinpoints of light we see in the world of deep space, a world that has never known either dawn or sunset.

Do we really know all there is to know about Comet Hale-Bopp? We've got the math right, but is math all there is? Is the trinity of number, weight, and measure enough to live by? Somehow, when I go out into the darkness of the backyard in the early evening and peer out past the big maple tree to find that fuzzy comet hanging apparently motionless in the sky below the constellation of Cassiopeia, I rather think not.

Here we are, on the downhill side of the winter solstice. The days are getting longer, at least according to the almanac. I'm not really sure, but it seems the dark is not quite so dark when I get up around six a.m.; maybe the difference is just the presence of the waning moon.

At that hour of the morning the moon seems a very different creature than the moon that rises some hours after sunset. For one thing, splendid as it may be when it is nearing full, the moon as it rises has to compete with the spectacular display of the going down of the greater light that rules the day.

In the early hours of the morning, though, the moon has the celestial stage all to itself. Not many of even the brightest stars can shine through the brightness of a full, or nearly full, moon. Then, the silvery light that spills into the windows on the southwest side of the house seems to be entirely its own—magical, fey, quite unlike the matter-of-fact, bluff, hearty daylight that will succeed it in an hour or two.

Someday I must really spend time learning something of the moon's language. It wasn't all that long ago I didn't know which way the horns of the moon pointed when it's waxing, or that they point the other way when it's waning; this, in spite of the fact that every calendar, which includes the phases of the moon, gives the orientation as plain as can be.

Next to the sun, of course, the moon is our most important near neighbour in space, the only celestial body, other than Earth, upon which a human foot has trod. Various spacecraft have passed near other of our planetary neighbours and sent back fascinating pictures of alien realms no human will likely ever visit. Only this month, the *National Geographic* published a series of pictures of the surface of Venus sent back by some sort of spacecraft with a radar scanner, which can pierce the heavy clouds that forever hide the surface of that planet from ordinary eyes.

Considering that the surface temperature of Venus is around 900 degrees, it will probably be forever inaccessible. And yet, we have seen photographs that show a landscape in such detail that I can imagine being able to walk around and pick up individual rocks from the ground. Here on Earth, unencumbered by immensely complicated scientific hardware, we know Venus as the "Star" that sometimes follows the sun at its setting, sometimes precedes it at its rising. Beautiful it is, beautiful, as was Wordsworth's Lucy:

Fair as a star, when only one
Is shining in the sky.

from "She Dwelt Among Untrodden Ways"

It's the moon above all that has drawn the thoughts and imaginations of people all down the ages. Before the dawn of history, sixteen hundred and more years before the time of Christ, people in what we now call the British Isles assembled lunar observatories. These arrangements of huge standing stones in the Orkneys and elsewhere enabled them to track the motions of the moon so accurately that they clearly knew of a slight perturbation in its orbit that was not to be discovered again until the time of Tycho Brahe in the sixteenth century of our era.

Of all the heavenly bodies, the moon wanders the most in its monthly journeys around Earth. Sometimes, when I get up in the early morning the moon is shining in the kitchen windows before disappearing behind the hill directly in back of us. At other times, it sets much further south along the ridge and is not visible in the kitchen windows at all. The sun, by contrast, also moves north and south in rising and setting but takes it a full year to make the journey from northernmost point to southernmost and back again.

Watchers of the moon have all sorts of wonderful terms that get into the almanacs. The moon is said to be "at apogee" or "at perigee." Sometimes it "rides high" and a week or so later it's said to "run low." One moment it's "at ascending node," which means it's beginning that part of its path through the heavens that takes it above the celestial equator. Not long after, it will be "at descending node."

I suppose its this wandering through the heavens, along with its waxing and waning, that makes the moon a symbol of inconstancy, as when Juliet says to Romeo,

O! swear not by the moon, the inconstant moon,
That monthly changes in her circled orb,
Lest that thy love prove likewise variable.

Inconstant or not, the moon has been a close companion down through the ages, a fit subject for folklore as well as for the most rarefied of scientific inquiry.

Chapter 11: Postlude

Winter has come in with a vengeance. More than long underwear weather, the temperature has been dropping steadily since mid-afternoon and now registers minus twelve Fahrenheit. The wind has picked up as well. I get out and put on the overalls, my down vest, the lumberjack coat, the knitted cap of an indestructible unknown fibre, and the leather mitts with knitted wool liners. I then struggle into boots with thick felt liners. (I momentarily recall the claustrophobic sense from childhood of being encased in a heavy snowsuit with all the trimmings.) Standing up, I open the inside kitchen door, pick up two water buckets, push open the aptly named storm door, and edge out onto the porch for the evening trip to the barn.

The cold air bites at me as it streams around the corner of the house. I think of finding a big muffler to wrap my neck and face. As I walk across the side porch carrying water to the cows, the decking complains loudly—creak, groan, creak…

I look out across the valley as I walk down the path to the barn. Lights, three miles away at the highway crossing and on farms along the valley, glow white and yellow, green and blue. They are always there, except when it is snowing hard. In the summer they have a friendly softness to them, but tonight they are points of sharp light with diamond edges, slicing through the snapping air.

Only a hundred yards or so separates house and barn. From the porch down to the big poplar trees, the path twists and turns through the snow so as to avoid the worst of the drifts piled up in the last storm. Come a storm or high wind and the path disappears like a camel track in the desert only to be re-invented in more-or-less the same place when the storm is over, or the wind has dropped.

The present path has lasted for several weeks. The snow has had its rough edges worn down from many trips to the barn until it is no more than a jumble sale of cast-offs underfoot. The snow sounds rubbery as I walk. It shifts unpredictably on the ice beneath it and can be treacherous to the unwary step.

Overhead, the sky is completely clear. The earth lies open to the black emptiness above it. The earth's heat is a raging furnace in comparison to the chill of outer space. Even so, my poor ears and nose feel the bite of the bitter cold. Moving away from the warm yellow light shining on the snow from the kitchen windows and trudging deeper into the dark, I am suddenly struck with a sense of tremendous loneliness.

On a night like this, earth's heat flows unhindered upward, up through this luxurious atmosphere we live in, up past thin air like that at the top of Mount Everest, and further still, past where the highest cirrus clouds can survive and into that strange region of the *aurora borealis* where it is blown away at last by the great wind of particles streaming past us off the sun into the blackness and emptiness of space. It seems cold comfort that this space, for all its emptiness, still holds a shred of hominess, lying as it does within the circle of the inner planets—Mercury, Venus, Earth and Mars—around a cozy star, and moving with it as part of one of the spiral arms of the galaxy we call the Milky Way.

But all the heat this earth respires into the void has no more effect on the almost absolute zero of even nearby space than the heat from our kitchen on the cold of our dooryard when I opened the doors to go out and closed them quickly behind me.

I shiver as I walk along, and the shiver is only partly the instinctive response of warm blood to cold air. The strangeness of all this tangle of things we call life and earth and home strikes more deeply than usual on a dark winter night.

A few months from now, when the grass and flowers of our Canadian spring almost explode from the ground, the air—filled with birds singing their strange sweet songs—will seem to enfold us and all living things in a blanket woven from many threads into a seamless tissue. Then, I think, it will be easy to be alive. Then, there will be no sense of boundary. Life, then flows on and our life flows with all life and life is all in all.

But this evening, in the deep of winter when the wind blows cold through the bare branches of the poplars above me, life seems a queer thing. When the atmosphere is so clear space has swallowed the sky, life seems a chance occurrence, the exception rather than the rule, and the shiver is partly a shiver of loneliness of this tiny spark in an ocean of cold.

I turn and cross the driveway above the chicken house, coming out from under the shadow of the trees into the clear air. I look up into the chilly blackness above the valley. Who can imagine such emptiness? Am I looking out or looking in? And then, suddenly, it happens.

There above me, a familiar figure, a pattern in the void draws my eye. Looking out or looking in, I wonder as emptiness organizes itself, ceases to be emptiness, links me to a home whose dooryard is all time and the starry heavens too.

A star map I saw as a child, dressed Orion in Roman garb: a short skirt, his left arm holding a lion skin as a kind of shield, a sword hanging from the stars of his belt, and a mighty club upraised against the bull who bears down on him from above. Now I just see the pattern of stars and above them, to the southwest, the V of the head of Taurus the Bull. And then, below him, to the southeast, I recognize Sirius, the Dog Star, the shining eye of Canis Major, Orion's faithful companion.

Between the chicken house and the barn, I pause. There in the sky, is all the glory of the starry heavens, shining as only they can when the air is cold and clear. Such a collection of wonders! I am warmed by a sense of oneness with others who, down through the ages, have looked into the night sky. I see and recognise Orion and the other now familiar presences twinkling against the black. There is Procyon, the other Dog Star, and Castor and Pollux, the heavenly twins. And there is bright Capella, and the Pleiades, the seven sisters, daughters of the Greek god Atlas and Pleione his wife; and below them this winter, and moving past them now, the unblinking stare of reddish Mars, god of war.

It's still bitterly cold and the wind stings tears from my eyes. Even in gloves my fingers are smarting with cold from grasping the handles of the water buckets. As I turn to finish my path, I wonder at the curious joy this chilly night has brought me.

I reach the door of the barn and go in to that smaller dark. With a flip of a switch the dark flees away, and blank emptiness becomes a familiar place. Thomas Not-a-Tom meets me as usual, purring. The other cats begin to appear: Cally, Spitz, Lopsie, and Queenie. Anka, the little heifer, sticks her nose over the top of her stall in greeting. From the other end of the floor comes the sound of clashing stanchions as Maggie and John Steer rise in expectation.

"Hello, Maggie," I say to my cow as I put a bucket of water in front of her and go to do the same for John Steer. Going back to the walkway, I open the big door behind John, take the shovel and begin to muck out.

About the Author

An academic throughout his early adulthood, Lee Whitney met his wife-to-be, Alice Willcox, in just that setting—a classroom at Cornell University. This serendipitous encounter marked the beginning of a mutual affinity that would form the basis for their future together.

After graduating in 1957 with a degree in English, Lee taught at a boys' school near Pittsburgh but returned to Cornell within twelve months, officially to start graduate work, but primarily for Alice. They were married in the fall of 1959 and relocated to southeast Virginia where Lee took a teaching position at Hampton Institute.

The Whitneys moved to Canada in 1962 where Lee began his licentiate at the Pontifical Institute of Medieval Studies (PIMS) in Toronto. While they never intended to stay in the city, a growing family made a teaching opportunity at Trinity College difficult to resist. Lee completed his Ph.D. at the University of Toronto and they remained in the city until 1977. Having acquired a summer property in rural New Brunswick two years prior, the Whitney family eventually settled there permanently.

In 1981, Lee was ordained an Anglican priest, taking responsibility for a small rural parish near Sussex. He would also return to teaching: religious studies at Mount Allison University, Chaucer at the University of New Brunswick, and, with Alice, English as a second language to newcomers.

Under the pen name, Jacob Erdman, Lee wrote a weekly column for the Kings County Record, in Sussex for 31 years. The column, *Letter from Home,* depicted daily life on the farm and the small events that lay at its centre. These stories, connected by present-time reflections, are the essence of Lee's book, *Knowing By Heart: A Tribute to a Kennebecasis Valley Homestead Farm.* It recounts the challenges and rewards of country life from the perspective of a couple who were blissfully unaware of the many surprises that farm life would bring.

Lee's fascination with weather led him to keep detailed records during their years on the farm. In 2013, the Fundy Biosphere Reserve created a video about his weather journals, as part of an initiative using citizen-sourced data to document climate change. The Fundy Biosphere Reserve received much praise for the film, which was on display at the Royal Ontario Museum, and which received peer validation through the Phoenix Award by the New Brunswick Environmental Network.

In 2014, Lee and Alice reluctantly said farewell to the farm and country life and relocated to Fredericton. Lee retired from the Kings County Record in 2016. They continue to appreciate the wonders of nature that they encounter on walks in the neighbourhood. Lee now shares his writings on his blog, often illustrated by Alice.

Both the blog and the video of the Whitney Journals can be found at www.jacoberdman.ca

About the Artwork and the Artists

The pastel painting on the front cover is by Alice Whitney. Alice also created the maps, and the flourishes used throughout the book.

Alice is a graduate of Cornell University with a degree in Fine Arts and has been a life-long practicing artist. She taught art at the high school in Sussex, New Brunswick for fourteen years and was a Charter Member of the Sussex Artist's Co-op (now called AX). Alice is the author and illustrator of *Henrietta's Nightlight*, which was shortlisted for the 2018 New Brunswick Book Award in the children's picture book category.

Lee and Alice Whitney's grandson, Stefan Westner created the prints for *Knowing By Heart*, adapting them from Alice's pastel paintings done during their years of living at the farm.

Stefan is a musician and visual artist. He is the organizer of the NB art collective *ShiftWork*; and co-founder of *FLOURISH*, a four-day music and art festival held annually in April in Fredericton, New Brunswick. Now working as a self-taught printmaker, Stefan's artistic journey started very early, at his grandmother's kitchen table.

Acknowledgements

Moving to our farm in the Kennebecasis Valley from Toronto was a big step; one that would not have been successful without the help of local people in the communities of Belleisle Creek, Springfield, Collina, and Kierstead Mountain who welcomed this odd family of newcomers into their midst. They taught us how to survive and thrive in the early days of our new life in rural New Brunswick. The names that stand out to us after all these years are Don and Mary Parlee, Rolph and Doris O'Neill, Anita French, Harold and Alma Parlee, Wes Alcorn, Floyd Rouse, and Willard Taylor.

And then there is the community of people, closer to our age, many of whom also arrived in New Brunswick from other places at about the same time we did and who became fast friends and helpmates: Paige and Marvin McDermott, Stephanie and Jerry Coburn, Pat and Chester Mercer, Peter and Stephanie de Graaf, and especially Sue Tyler and Clark Phillips who were mentors to most of us "back-to-the-landers."

Once I started writing columns for the *Kings County Record*, I appreciated each and every editor I worked with over more than thirty years. My thanks to Ann Farrell, who started this whole thing; and to Jamie Roach, Giselle McKnight, Tammy Scott-Wallace, and to others whose names I have forgotten—my thanks to you all. My weekly columns started as a typewritten paper copy, dropped off by Alice on Wednesday mornings on her way to teach school. Eventually they came to be transmitted through the ether by electronic wizardry. I knew not then and still don't know how such things happen, but I am grateful to all who make systems like this work for writers.

There are so many more that we remember fondly and owe gratitude to, it's impossible to mention them all!

www.ingramcontent.com/pod-product-compliance
Lightning Source LLC
Chambersburg PA
CBHW070458200726
48293CB00007B/2275

* 9 7 8 1 9 8 8 2 9 9 2 7 3 *